First published in Great Britain

2022 by Jack Soley

This publication is the second edition published in 2025.

Copyright © Jack Soley, 2022

Jack Soley has asserted his moral right to be identified as the Author of this work in accordance with the Copyright Designs and Patents Act 1988.

All rights reserved. No part of this publication may be reproduced, stored in a retrieval system, or transmitted in any form or by any means, electronic, mechanical, photocopying, recording or otherwise, without the prior permission of the publisher.

A catalogue record for this book is available from the British Library.

All opinions are of that of the author and do not represent the views of the publishing company or their affiliates.

This book is published by Pomerak Ventures Ltd, registered in England & Wales under the company number 15578139.

ISBN: 9781917706018

Contents

Prologue 8

North America 12

    Canada 13

    Dominican Republic 17

    Mexico 19

    Nicaragua 23

    United States of America 25

South America 34

    Argentina 35

    Bolivia 38

    Brazil 40

    Chile 43

    Colombia 46

    Ecuador 48

    Peru 50

    Uruguay 53

    Venezuela 55

Europe 57

    Albania 58

    Belgium 60

- Cyprus 62
- Denmark 64
- France 66
- Germany 68
- Greece 70
- Ireland 72
- Italy 74
- Poland 76
- Portugal 78
- Russia 80
- Spain 82
- United Kingdom 86

Asia 92
- (People's Republic of) China 93
- India 99
- Indonesia 101
- Iran 103
- Israel 107
- Japan 109
- Jordan 111
- Kazakhstan 113
- Malaysia 115

    Mongolia 118

    Oman 120

    Pakistan 122

    Philippines 124

    Qatar 126

    Taiwan (Republic of China) 128

    Türkiye 130

    Vietnam 134

    Yemen 136

Africa 139

    Algeria 140

    Botswana 142

    Cabo Verde 144

    Egypt 146

    Kenya 148

    Madagascar 150

    Mauritania 155

    Morocco 157

    Mozambique 159

    Namibia 161

    Nigeria 164

    Senegal 166

South Africa 168

Tunisia 179

Oceania 184

Australia 185

Fiji 197

New Zealand 199

Vanuatu 202

Honourable Mentions 205

Final Thoughts 208

References 210

Prologue

This time last year, my first book, entitled "The Sandboarding Book", made its way onto bookshelves. The book was available for purchase; the book enjoyed moderate success, bagging mentions on sports blogs that weren't my own and scoring interviews on a few media outlets. I was incredibly proud of accomplishing something I saw as worthwhile with my time, and I began to witness a genuine interest in the sport I had spent many years trying to promote.

A year has passed, and if you've read the previous book, you'll realise that I mentioned a future book about all the places you can try out Sandboarding. But, I won't lie; it wasn't long after the initial work was published that I caught what I could only describe as the 'writers bug' where I made a book, and I wanted to make another, so here I am.

I encourage many people to visit these places in this book, in their home country; or opposite the world. I haven't been to most of the destinations I'll be listing, and everything will be sourced by referencing and experiences from other eager travelling folks. Data listed will include snippets such as nations' data about the country's crime rate or cost of living or details of how vast the dunes are once you arrive. I praised this website in the previous book, and I shall praise it here: Numbeo.com is a crowd-sourced website that collects figures regarding health care, crime rates, cost of living, and quality of life among other indices.

I shall be including those statistics, as well the visa policy for citizens of the United Kingdom (as it's my home country); United States (as a lot of readers of my blog are from there); and Israel (as I know some countries will make it difficult for Israelis to enter and a lot of my blog readership hails from Israel). The information I'll acquire the visa requirements information will be from a website I also use regularly, visalist.io. All visa information was researched and compiled on the 29th June 2022. Where I've mentioned that an entry visa isn't required, this doesn't take into consideration if there's any entry fees payable. These requirements are strictly for tourist visas, when this book hits the shelves, the visa policies of the countries in the book may change, and where a time frame for visas is not listed, it doesn't always mean it's for an indefinite time, so check it. I'm listing the visa rules at the time of publication and to be safe, you should double check with the consulate or embassy of the country you're planning to visit.

I used to mention the relevant country's position on the "World Happiness Report, " an annual publication from the United Nations measuring quality of life. If citizens feel happy in their home country, I've scrapped this index as I believe a crowd-sourced index that measured quality of life would give a more accurate representation of the people who live in other countries. I also used to include the internet speed of the relevant nations, I've stopped including this as more and more people can access the internet and as infrastructure gets more advanced, it would just come naturally that more people can access the world wide web.

And before I begin this journey, I will not be ranking the countries as I go along, I will be simply listing the dunes that I've found in the country and providing relevant statistics that may make the country more appealing to keen travelers, like us. I take great consideration to mention as many places as I possibly can per country. Unless the nation in question is bombarded with dunes perfect for Sandboarding, I've done my best to include countries you wouldn't typically associate with this burgeoning sport. I also can't guarantee that all of these dunes will be open to recreation; as governments change rules, a sand dune complex may suddenly be transformed into a nature reserve and all public access be restricted or limited. I'm acting on information which is general knowledge at the time of publication. This book might be the Top 100 destinations, there is no order or rank but they're my Top 100 for sure.

Now I've laid out the rules of how I'll be listing all the places in this book, I hope that wherever you plan to be heading you'll make a wise and informed decision given the information I've included in this book, I hope you'll see this as more than "just a travel book" but an informative and comprehensive global guide of the world's greatest Sandboarding destinations.

North America

As previously unearthed in the last book, you don't have to have an arid and dusty desert to enjoy sandboarding; North America isn't just home to harsh landscapes like those in Baja California and the continental U.S. but also the freezing wilderness of Canada & Alaska. The aim of these continental chapters is to advertise countries that aren't commonly thought to have sand dunes in their borders. In all honesty, North America will be a bit of a struggle as most of the nations I've included here would have a suitable environment for dunes. Still, hopefully, I've featured countries that aren't those that aren't traditionally known for the sport. If you noticed, in the last book, I included a few volcanoes into the mix (I know it's technically a Sandboarding, not a Volcano boarding book, but it's close enough).

Canada

Crime Rate: 42.95 (lowest in North America)

Cost of Living Index: 70.22 (highest in North America)

Quality of Life Index: 160.38

Health Care Index: 71.31

Visa requirement for US citizens: No visa required for 6 months

Visa requirement for UK citizens: E-visa valid for 6 months

Visa requirement for Israel citizens: E-visa valid for 6 months

Canada is known for snowboarding, so much so that since the sport was introduced to the 1998 Winter Olympics, Canada has won 17 medals, 5 being gold. (Olympanalyt, n.d.)

Sandboarding is making a small footprint on Canadian sports, and rightly so! Some parts of Canada are perfect for hitting the dunes; one of them is a previous inclusion in the last book, the Carcross Desert. The Carcross Desert isn't a place that's been unheard of before my book; locals are well aware that the keen sportsperson will happily come here. "*In summer, exposed dunes are used by quad bikers, hikers and sand-boarders, and become a shelter for dall sheep, mountain goats and deer.*" (MacEacheran, M. 2018)

"Carcross desert 2 (1189913080)" by John Johnston is licensed under CC BY 2.0.

Over in Quebec, the Tadoussac dunes are geared for those who love a bit of nature with their extreme sports; this area offers panoramic views of the St. Lawrence, which on good days, you will be able to spot whales from the dunes; these dunes according to the MTL Blog are:

"*one of the three prime whale-watching points in the Tadoussac area.*" (MacDonald, T. 2020) It's a valuable snippet of knowledge that camping here isn't allowed.

"Tadoussac Sand Dunes (39223396261)" by Mindmatrix is licensed under CC BY-SA 2.0.

The final stop in Canada is the Great Sand Hills of Saskatchewan; this is one of the many places around the world that proves that great sand dunes need not exist in a dry and uninhabitable desert. This region also has a ban on camping and fires, and a very moving quote is found on the website from the Saskatchewan tourism board, which instructs those to "take only pictures, leave only footprints." Atlas Obscura has noted that: "*These dunes are very lightly visited, and many western Canadians don't even know they exist.*" (Atlas Obscura, 2014)

"Shifting Dunes" by Drm310 is licensed under CC BY-SA 2.0.

Dominican Republic

Crime Rate: 60.94 (highest in North America)

Cost of Living Index: 41.77

Quality of Life Index: Not Known

Health Care Index: 55.55 (lowest in North America)

Visa requirement for US citizens: No visa required for 1 month

Visa requirement for UK citizens: No visa required for 1 month

Visa requirement for Israel citizens: No visa required for 3 months

It's not one of the most scenic countries, I'll admit, and when it comes to Sandboarding, it's mostly overlooked. However, I did feature the Dunas De Bani sand dunes an hour from the nation's capital, Santo Domingo. Although, the tallest of these dunes is 35 metres high, it is a wise idea to take plenty of water, as Jade from We Travel And Blog says: *"To visit you have to try to go as early in the morning as possible because, with no shade in sight, the sand get very hot, very fast."* (Adele, J. n.d.)

"Dunas de Baní 1" by Ronny Medina is licensed under CC BY 4.0.

Mexico

Crime Rate: 53.68

Cost of Living Index: 35.35 (lowest in North America)

Quality of Life Index: 124.9

Health Care Index: 72.83 (highest in North America)

Visa requirement for US citizens: No visa required for 6 months

Visa requirement for UK citizens: No visa required for 6 months

Visa requirement for Israel citizens: No visa required for 6 months

With a booming tourism industry and many visitors flocking to visit Cancún each year, the North of Mexico and, to a lesser extent, Baja California, where the first of these dunes can be found: The Dunas de San Felipe. To quote the Ministry of Tourism of Baja California: "*The Dunes of San Felipe are formations of white sand. The characteristics of its environment offer optimal conditions for tourism adventures. Close to the dunes there are ideal sites for practicing alpinism and cross country cycling.*" (Ministry of Tourism of Baja California, n.d.) You can reach the dunes on a single road from the town of Mexicali on the U.S.-Mexico border. From that road, you can also find the Dunas de la Pintas, used to film the James Bond film, Quantum of Solace. There are many sites for Baja California, so I used an image of dunes in Baja California to give a rough impression of what the landscape looks like.

"Mexicali, Baja California (20445916293)" by Comisión Mexicana de Filmaciones is licensed under CC BY-SA 2.0.

Still, in Mexico, the Salamayuca Dune Fields in Chihuahua, which borders Texas, is another sandboarding site of great interest for many people; and another place for movie buffs as the 1984 movies Dune and Conan The Destroyer had scenes that were filmed here. The dunes of Salamayuca are adjacent to Federal Highway 45, which runs through the town of Salamayuca.

"Mostrando el Record Guinness" by Techmaster4444 is licensed under CC BY-SA 3.0.

And finally, we travel to the east coast of the country, where we end up in Veracruz, where the dunes on the beach town of Playa Chachalacas; it's five hours from Mexico City, and oddly enough, the top activity here is, in fact, fishing. The dunes are often explored by hiking, paragliding, and sandboarding; The water sports here make it a haven no matter what sport takes your fancy.

"Dunas del Sabanal, Chachalaca, Veracruz (23663560362)" by Comisión Mexicana de Filmaciones is licensed under CC BY-SA 2.0.

Nicaragua

Crime Rate: 47.89

Cost of Living Index: 39.64

Quality of Life Index: Not Known

Health Care Index: Not Known

Visa requirement for US citizens: No visa required for 3 months

Visa requirement for UK citizens: No visa required for 3 months

Visa requirement for Israel citizens: No visa required for 3 months

Nicaragua's sandboarding scene is dominated by one site, and it's not even definitively a sand dune by a volcano. You may recall from my first book that Nicaragua became a hotspot for Sandboarding in 1999 when the volcano erupted, and the mixture of hardened lava and ashes made sandboarding possible. Described as *"Central America's youngest volcano was born in April 1850 and is one of the region's most active volcanoes."* (Volcano Discovery, 2022) In its 172-year existence, it has erupted 24 times, averaging an eruption every 7 years. Luckily the area isn't near significant populations, but the volcano poses risks to farmland and rural regions.

"Volcano Boarding Cerro Negro" by NicaPlease is a public domain work.

United States of America

Crime Rate: 48.16

Cost of Living Index: 70.13

Quality of Life Index: 170.72 (highest in North America)

Health Care Index: 69.06

Visa requirement for US citizens: None, because you're American.

Visa requirement for UK citizens: E-visa valid for 3 months

Visa requirement for Israel citizens: Visa required

If you've read the last book, you will likely see that the United States is one of the contenders for where Sandboarding in its modern form was invented. It's no surprise that because the United States landscape is so large, there are plenty of top spots to hit the dunes; I'll start with a dune that I didn't discuss in the last book. Pismo Beach is not too far from the settlement of Oceano, "*The Oceano sand dune area is recognized by scientists, conservationists, government agencies, and the public as the finest, most extensive coastal dunes remaining in California.*" (Experience Pismo Beach, n.d.) These dunes, aside from sports, are also a good place for fishing, digging for clams, and horse riding.

"Oceano dunes beach" by Ken Figlioli is licensed under CC BY-SA 2.0.

Up next is somewhere where I knew dunes would exist, but I thought I'd discuss this place in this book; in Death Valley National Park lives the Mesquite Flat Sand Dunes, and no, they're not flat at all! I have included these dunes nearby; they're the only few dunes where Sandboarding is allowed. There's no official trail on these dunes; a round trip to the tallest dune and back to the entry point will take around 1 and a half hours. The National Parks Service clearly states that the "*Eureka, Hidden, Panamint Valley, and Ibex Sand Dune Systems are closed to sledding, sand boarding and sand skiing to protect the federally listed plant species and other sensitive endemic flora and fauna. Sand boarding is permitted at Mesquite and Saline Sand Dunes.*" (National Park Service, n.d.) Stay mindful that it's not advised to hike after 10am in the summer due to the high heat, and pets are off limits even if you're carrying them.

"Mesquite Flat Sand Dunes 1989 09" by LBM1948 is licensed under CC BY-SA 4.0.

Staying in California, the Dumont Dunes is an area of the greater Mojave Desert that is awash, with many people riding ATVs throughout the year. You will need to buy a permit to visit the dunes; some rules are strictly enforced, for instance, shooting is not allowed, glass containers are not allowed, no trash dumping and camping is permitted; however, it can't block a route and can't be any longer than 14 days. These dunes are used mainly by street legal and off-road ATVs; they lie just outside Death Valley National Park, so be careful of the blistering heat.

"Dumont Dunes at Sunrise" by Bureau of Land Management California is a public domain work.

Another dune region that I wanted to mention in the last book but shall now include in my Top 100 list is the Great Sand Dunes National Park in Colorado; the park area is 3 times larger than all of the sand dunes in England & Wales. "*Sandboarding, sledding, and skiing are permitted anywhere on the dunefield away from vegetated areas. From the main Dunes Parking Area, it's a minimum 0.7 mile (1km) hike to get to the small or medium-sized slopes; the top of the first high ridge is 1.25 miles. Smaller slopes at the base are fine for young children, while teens and adults may prefer longer slopes near the top of the first high ridge of dunes.*" (National

Park Service, n.d.) Other advice is that spring afternoons are windy, and you should try to hit the dunes in the early morning or evening to avoid the dunes that allegedly have a surface temperature of 150 degrees Fahrenheit.

"Great Sand Dunes National Park - dunes, view to south" by Pimlico27 is licensed under CC BY-SA 4.0.

The final 2 dunes for the USA are the ones I mentioned in the last book; the first is the Coral Pink Sand Dunes

State Park in Utah, the daily fee required for entry on the dunes can be purchased in person or online. "All of the dunes are open for hiking and kid-friendly playing. You can rent sand boards and sand sleds onsite. About 90-percent of the dunes are open for off-highway vehicles (OHV), a popular park attraction." (Visit Utah, n.d.) These dunes were formed because of the erosion of nearby sandstone cliffs, estimated to be around 10,000 to 15,000 years old. This park was first opened to the public in 1963.

"Coral pink sand dunes 01" by Samulili is licensed under CC BY 2.0.

And the final top sandboarding spot in the United States undoubtedly puts the sport of Sandboarding on the map, the world's first purpose-built Sandboarding park. "*While the 40-acre park is constantly changing thanks to the nomadic nature of the dunes, just down Highway 101 is Oregon Dunes Recreation Area with its more than 27,000 acres of dunes to explore. Each year it's estimated more than two million people visit the dunes on the southern Oregon coast.*" (Johnson, P. n.d.) So again, I commend the owner, Lon Beale, a big inspiration of mine, for making this park a reality, this park caters to every skill level, and the only thing you need to worry about is rain.

"Oregon Dunes (5869952434)" by John Fowler is licensed under CC BY 2.0.

South America

When I wrote the first book, I knew the countries that the dunes were in, but I wasn't aware of the number of sand dunes in these countries, and now I've done this book, I've added more countries to what I'd consider "my list". From what I've seen about South America, it's not necessarily safe from crime, but from what I do know, it's surprisingly welcoming to tourists, particularly those from the English-speaking world, not to mention that the Sandboarding scene is by far the liveliest and most enthusiastic on the planet. The deserts here are mostly dry and somewhat cold, but sand dunes don't have to be in deserts, right? A lot of these dunes will surprise you as to where they are.

Argentina

Crime Rate: 64.14

Cost of Living Index: 34.69

Quality of Life Index: 105.42

Health Care Index: 69.32 (highest in South America)

Visa requirement for US citizens: No visa required for 3 months

Visa requirement for UK citizens: No visa required for 3 months

Visa requirement for Israel citizens: No visa required for 3 months

As the nation that calls itself the "Land of Silver", the dunes here aren't that many, but their quality makes them worthy as a land of gold in my eyes. In South America, many focus on more significant countries for the Sandboarding scene, and many visit other nations such as Chile and Brazil. The Dunes of Tatón in Catamarca Province aren't all too known, and there's little documented information on these dunes, but there's more information on the nearby Federico Kirbus Dune. "*Duna Federico Kirbus in Argentina is the highest sand dune in the world, standing at a whopping 4035ft tall.*"

(Original Travel, n.d.) To put this dune into perspective, it's taller than the tallest peak in 53 countries.

"La Duna de Randolfo, camino a Antofgagasta de la Sierra, Catamarca, Argentina - panoramio" by rodoluca is licensed under CC BY-SA 3.0.

What if I told you that there was a part of Argentina that speaks Welsh? Well, in Chubut Province, around 5,000 people use the language, it's an official minority language of the province, and in the town of Puerto Madryn, the Welsh dragon appears on its town flag. Aside from the sand dunes you can surf on, there are many opportunities for whale watching, looking out for penguins, and even having Welsh tea in the many towns nearby. Most of the dunes are in Puerto Madryn, but you will find a lot of smaller dunes around the coast of Chubut too.

"Cerro avanzado" by Gonce is licensed under CC BY-SA 4.0.

Bolivia

Crime Rate: 58.28

Cost of Living Index: 34.77

Quality of Life Index: Not Known

Health Care Index: Not Known

Visa requirement for US citizens: Visa on arrival for 1 month

Visa requirement for UK citizens: No visa required for 3 months

Visa requirement for Israel citizens: Visa required

Bolivia is one of two landlocked countries in South America, it's one of the highest altitude countries on the planet, and in many Sandboarding reference works, this country needs to make the lists. Notable sights include the El Camino De La Muerte (The Death Road) and the world's largest salt flat; a sandboarding destination in this country is the "El Parque Regional Lomas de Arena" near the city of Santa Cruz de la Sierra. Although these dunes are some of the best in all of Bolivia, there isn't too much infrastructure for tourists and assaults on tourists aren't unheard of; one thing is sure is that it wasn't the dune that was the main attraction. "*The main attraction of this tourist destination used to be the immense lagoon that existed in the center of the main sand hills. But now instead of water there are only pampas and bushes."* (Amboro Tours, n.d.)

"Lomas de Arena - Santa Cruz, Bolivia" by Gabriel Millos is licensed under CC BY-SA 2.0.

Brazil

Crime Rate: 67.01

Cost of Living Index: 33.24

Quality of Life Index: 107.04

Health Care Index: 57.84

Visa requirement for US citizens: No visa required for 3 months

Visa requirement for UK citizens: No visa required for 3 months

Visa requirement for Israel citizens: No visa required for 3 months

I mentioned 2 popular sandboarding spots in my last book in Brazil; no other dune regions can compare to the Florianopolis dunes and the Lençóis Maranhenses National Park for Sandboarding in this incredibly diverse country. I'll start off with the Florianopolis dunes; it's worth mentioning that according to Lost Towel Travels: "*Anyone who has already sand boarded in Huacachina in Peru or is planning to travel there later will most likely give this a miss since the dunes surrounding the Peruvian oasis are much taller.*" (Lost Towel Travels, 2021) Don't get me wrong, the dunes of Florianopolis are nothing to be sniffed at; these dunes have been used by Brazilian athletes for training and tourists hoping to get their sandboarding fix.

"Sand dunes in Florianópolis 3" by Mx. Granger is a public domain work.

The Lençóis Maranhenses National Park is home to a vast volume of lagoons and sand dunes that traverse the landscape for miles and miles afar. The best thing to do if you don't have a Sandboard of your own is to see if you can hire one in the nearby town of Barreirinhas. It's critical to be aware that "*There are no campgrounds or amenities in the park, so visitors spend the night in Barreirinhas and nearby towns. In this region, you can find basic accommodation like pousadas as well as more upscale hotels and resorts."* (Ribeiro, P. 2021) For those who don't know, a pousada is the same as a boutique hotel or hostel.

"Lençois Maranhenses - Walking" by Dlaurini is licensed under CC BY-SA 4.0.

Chile

Crime Rate: 53.98

Cost of Living Index: 43.9

Quality of Life Index: 100.15

Health Care Index: 63.97

Visa requirement for US citizens: No visa required for 3 months

Visa requirement for UK citizens: No visa required for 3 months

Visa requirement for Israel citizens: No visa required for 3 months

So the veteran Sandboarders will know that Chile is home to the Atacama Desert and some of the most impressive dunes on the South American continent, if not the world. Iquique is the 7th most populated urban area in Chile, it's home to one of two freeports in the country, and the "Cerro Dragon" or Dragon Hill towers over the city below, "*Varying in height from 150 to 500 meters, it is the largest urban sand dune in the world; only the dunes of the Sahara are higher. The dune is situated on a narrow rocky ledge above a cliff 500 feet high that forms a natural barrier to the sea.*" (Patowary, K. 2014)

"Vista del Cerro Dragón desde la carretera que conecta a Iquique con Alto Hospicio." by Freddy Alexander Bugueño Tolmo is licensed under CC BY-SA 3.0.

My book is limited to 100 places, so I won't dwell on Chile, as I could mention a few more. I'd like to discuss the dunes of San Pedro de Atacama, given that this once-Spanish colonial town is quite remote compared to where most people live in Chile. The Flamencos National Park that borders Bolivia and Argentina is a haven for caverns that excite, canyons that intrigue, and, naturally, Sandboarding. In the nearby Valley of the Dead, Ecochile reports: "*This valley is the perfect place to sandboard. The Valley of the Moon also has a huge sand dune but you are not allowed to sandboard on it. As well as climbing the dune to ride back down, it is also worth going up for the view alone. The desert rolls out before your eyes, stretching all the way to the jagged Andes mountains, cowboys ride through the rugged valleys, kicking up dust in their wake, and bizarre outcrops defy logic at every turn."* (Ecochile, 2017)

"Dune Quebrada de Quisma - Valle de la Muerte - SPA - panoramio" by Roberto Ortuzar is licensed under CC BY 3.0.

Colombia

Crime Rate: 57.71

Cost of Living Index: 26.72 (lowest in South America)

Quality of Life Index: 103.54

Health Care Index: 67.19

Visa requirement for US citizens: No visa required for 3 months

Visa requirement for UK citizens: No visa required for 3 months

Visa requirement for Israel citizens: No visa required for 6 months

On the continent, Colombia is often left behind in the Sandboarding scene. To say that Sandboarding isn't a thing in Colombia couldn't be further from the truth; the coastline of the Caribbean Sea is dominated by the dunes on the shore; nearby kitesurfing is a dominant sport in the town of Cabo de la Vela. However, the Dunes of Taroa aren't known for their Sandboarding; "*Colombia's wild northeast is slowly making its way onto the tourist map. But patience and a fair dose of discomfort are required to enjoy this barren outpost. Accommodation is basic and extremely limited.*" (Nicolson, N. 2015)

"Dunas de Taroa" by Uhkabu is licensed under CC BY-SA 3.0.

Ecuador

Crime Rate: 57.24

Cost of Living Index: 37.34

Quality of Life Index: 118.84

Health Care Index: 69.26

Visa requirement for US citizens: No visa required for 3 months

Visa requirement for UK citizens: No visa required for 3 months

Visa requirement for Israel citizens: No visa required for 3 months

One of the smallest countries on the continent, this country is literally called Equator because, if you haven't guessed, that's where it sits on the planet; you could be fearless and attempt to do volcano boarding down Chimborazo or Cotopaxi, or you could take a visit to the Palmira Desert which is still in Chimborazo province, Zenith Travel explains this little desert perfectly: "*It is a very small desert, in no way comparable to other larger deserts such as those located in Peru, Bolivia, Chile or the famous Sahara. But what makes it very special is the contrast that can be found between the sand dunes, the pine forests and the authentic indigenous communities that live around it."* (Zenith Travel, 2022.) Of course, Sandboarding is allowed here, but the same article even admits that the dunes of Peru & Chile are more significant, but it wins a place in this book because it's somewhere different.

"Erosioenparamo" by Patomena is a public domain work.

Peru

Crime Rate: 67.1

Cost of Living Index: 32.53

Quality of Life Index: 80.42

Health Care Index: 56.2

Visa requirement for US citizens: No visa required for 3 months

Visa requirement for UK citizens: No visa required for 6 months

Visa requirement for Israel citizens: No visa required for 3 months

This place is where a lot of Sandboarding in South America takes place, and if Sandboarding was a country, Peru would probably be its capital. One of the tall sandy hills where the sport regularly occurs is Cerro Blanco, both of these top Peruvian Sandboarding spots are in the Ica department, so you don't have to go cross-country to get your session off the ground. According to Peruvian legend: "*a beautiful princess took a dip in a beautiful pool but was interrupted by a young man who ran into her while she bathed. She was startled, grabbed her clothes, and fled. When she ran, she created the famous sand dunes with her mantle as she crossed through the desert.*

She dragged her cape behind her and created Cerro Blanco." (Luna, M. 2021)

"Cerro Blanco near La Huaca de la Luna- Ice cream seller" by Thayne Tuason is licensed under CC BY 4.0.

Suppose you travel 3 hours north in a car from Cerro Blanco or 4 hours south in a vehicle from Lima. In that case, you'll end up in Huacachina, which is undoubtedly the hub of all Sandboarding in South America, if not, a great contender. I have praised this area often online and in print; when talking about the site's climate, *"Huacachina's weather is consistently warm and sunny, and the area rarely experiences rain. This means travelers can visit the charming village any time of the year. However, the best time to explore Huacachina is between April and July, as the temperatures averages at 67°F."* (Auma, Q. 2022)

"Laguna de la huacachina 2" by Jonathan Marco Corredor Obispo is licensed under CC BY-SA 4.0.

Uruguay

Crime Rate: 51.44 (lowest in South America)

Cost of Living Index: 52.07 (highest in South America)

Quality of Life Index: 122.26 (highest in South America)

Health Care Index: 68.36

Visa requirement for US citizens: No visa required for 3 months

Visa requirement for UK citizens: No visa required for 3 months

Visa requirement for Israel citizens: No visa required for 3 months

Uruguay is one of the most intriguing countries on the South American continent. Uruguay was once part of Brazil, but it speaks Spanish. I remember learning a little bit about the country in school, and I distinctly remember making an article about the dunes of Cabo Polonio back in my blogging heyday. Cabo Polonio is isolated and cut off from the rest of Uruguay as there aren't any roads, and that makes it a good spot for urban dwellers to flock in the Cisplatine summer when it comes to the dunes: "*it's an actual national park, protected territory, and all visitors are encouraged to do their best to keep it clean and pristine.*" (Ellis, D. 2019) Like everywhere else, I encourage you to take your trash home and leave the dunes as you found them.

"Caminata a la tarde(Cabo Polonio)" by Jorgestenopeico is licensed under CC BY-SA 3.0.

Venezuela

Crime Rate: 83.58 (highest in this book)

Cost of Living Index: 43.2

Quality of Life Index: 77.43 (lowest in South America)

Health Care Index: 39.31 (lowest in this book)

Visa requirement for US citizens: Visa required

Visa requirement for UK citizens: No visa required for 3 months

Visa requirement for Israel citizens: Visa required

I'll be frank, I had no idea that Sandboarding was a thing in Venezuela. Most of the news about the country is dominated by its politics, monetary policies, and poor circumstances that lead to its high crime rates and low quality of life compared to the rest of the continent. The dunes in the Médanos De Coro National Park are near the Paraguaná peninsula: "*Many pirates and smugglers sought refuge on the peninsula in colonial times. Today, the area is popular with tourists and oil companies.*" (NASA Earth Observatory, n.d.) the area is also popular with horse riding, quad biking, and camel rides if horses aren't your thing; if you're looking to get here from Caracas, it'll be around 500 kilometres by road.

"Medanos de Coro - Edo. Falcon" by Oliver J. Bello is licensed under CC BY-SA 3.0.

Europe

As one of the most developed places on the planet, it looks green from a satellite image, but you have beaches, a few rocky mountain regions here and there, and dunes do exist in some hidden places. The benefit of Europe is that everything is well connected and you're not always too far away from a central town or city. Sandboarding has taken off in Europe in the last few years, and hopefully even more so in some countries that I didn't know had dunes until I wrote this book. If there was one continent I never expected to have as many dunes as I thought, it'd be this one.

Albania

Crime Rate: 46.08

Cost of Living Index: 35.5

Quality of Life Index: Not Known

Health Care Index: 50.54 (lowest in Europe)

Visa requirement for US citizens: No visa required for 3 months

Visa requirement for UK citizens: No visa required for 3 months

Visa requirement for Israel citizens: No visa required for 3 months

I certainly had not considered Albania when it comes to Sandboarding in European countries; admittedly, there's a lot of focus on more western European nations. One of the aims of this book is to market some of the best dunes worldwide regardless of where national borders lie. The literal translation of this place is "thrown sand"; the small beach of Rana E Hedhun isn't too far from the border with Montenegro and only an hour's drive from Shkodër, Albania's 5th largest city by population. Not a lot is known about these dunes, but the dunes are directly near the sea, so if you plan to surf these sands, do it at low tide.

"Rana e hedhun" by Albinfo is licensed under CC BY-SA 4.0.

Belgium

Crime Rate: 45.38

Cost of Living Index: 72.61

Quality of Life Index: 151.86

Health Care Index: 75.49

Visa requirement for US citizens: No visa required for 3 months

Visa requirement for UK citizens: No visa required for 3 months

Visa requirement for Israel citizens: No visa required for 3 months

It's a big surprise that I'd include a country that's part of the traditional low countries. Belgium is home to the town of De Panne and the nearby Bray Dunes, which also sit on the border with France. So you can sandboard from Belgium and end up in France and vice versa. The elephant in the room is that these dunes are tiny; in most parts, they rise less than 10 metres above the sea. I've included these because for small children and those looking to start out, it's a perfect place to start to get a feel for your balance; the low speeds and small distance make it ideal for a complete novice. Also, by sandboarding in De Panne and Bray Dunes, you could cross an invisible border, so you could tell people that you managed to train for a sport in 2 countries on the same day.

"RNN de la dune Marchand entre Braye-Dunes et Zuytcoote (41)" by PIERRE ANDRE LECLERCQ is licensed under CC BY-SA 4.0.

Cyprus

Crime Rate: 32.12

Cost of Living Index: 59.03

Quality of Life Index: 147.1

Health Care Index: 51.98

Visa requirement for US citizens: No visa required for 3 months

Visa requirement for UK citizens: No visa required for 3 months

Visa requirement for Israel citizens: No visa required for 3 months

Legally speaking, this spot is within the British base area of Akrotiri, but you'll have to pass through Cyprus if you arrive by civilian aircraft so make of this what you will, but here lie sand dunes in the so-called "Limassol Desert". "*The sand dunes are close to the southernmost tip of the Akrotiri peninsula and are accessible to the public only via a sketchy dirt road. And the unusual grey colour of the sand here is what makes the dunes particularly unique. Shadows created by the dunes form a dreamlike setting, dissimilar to anything else visitors will see in the region.*" (Agathangelou, C. 2017) Limassol, which is Cyprus' 2nd largest city, isn't far from the dunes, so once you've had a day on the sands, you can relax with the many hotspots the city offers.

"Dunes Sand Sky" by dimitrisvetsikas1969 is a public domain work.

Denmark

Crime Rate: 26.56 (lowest in Europe)

Cost of Living Index: 84.12 (highest in Europe)

Quality of Life Index: 192.36 (highest in this book)

Health Care Index: 80.07

Visa requirement for US citizens: No visa required for 3 months

Visa requirement for UK citizens: No visa required for 3 months

Visa requirement for Israel citizens: No visa required for 3 months

I knew this book was bound to be biased as the colder countries wouldn't commonly be mentioned as often; however, in Denmark, a particular sand dune warrants a mention. This inclusion also helps that Denmark once topped my blog's annual "Top 10 Sandboarding Countries" list. Rubjerg Knude isn't home to a sandboarding scene, but if you want to hit the dunes here, you'll find the dunes that perch over the Skaggerak that are a by-product of shifting sands and coastal erosion. These dunes once engulfed a lighthouse that has now been moved further inland to put the scale of the decay into perspective: "*When the 23-metre Rubjerg Knude lighthouse was first lit in 1900 in northern Jutland, Denmark, it was roughly 200 metres away from the coast. Over the years, that distance shrank to six metres and the lighthouse was predicted to fall into the sea by 2023, together with the cliff on which it stood."* (Dora, V.D. 2022) So if you want to board here, do it fast and carefully!

"Rubjerg Knude Lighthouse - Jutland municipality of Hjørring in Northern Denmark - 13 June 2014" by Nelson L is licensed under CC BY 2.0.

France

Crime Rate: 52.41 (highest in Europe)

Cost of Living Index: 74.13

Quality of Life Index: 156.65

Health Care Index: 80.18 (highest in Europe)

Visa requirement for US citizens: No visa required for 3 months

Visa requirement for UK citizens: No visa required for 3 months

Visa requirement for Israel citizens: No visa required for 3 months

I have been to this next destination to make it look like I've done some reporting for this book. The Dune of Pilat is not far from Bordeaux and is open to families for a day on the beach, paragliding, surfing, or sandboarding. Sadly in 2022, the forest near the dune caught ablaze and the dune itself was closed for a prolonged period. I visited in the autumn of 2022, and there was a sign that outright banned board sports; however, on certain days, I would suspect that events would be held, and I did see a lot of other activities take place on the dunes. As mentioned in my first book, I still need concrete evidence that sandboarding on the side facing the forest is forbidden.

Still, with the summer wildfires that Europe is sadly experiencing much of lately, I wouldn't even bother to attempt it. Even if you come here for a day on the dunes, bring plenty of water because, given the sheer size of this area, you will need it.

"Dune du pyla 2009" by Pline is licensed under CC BY-SA 2.0.

Germany

Crime Rate: 36.37

Cost of Living Index: 65.58

Quality of Life Index: 180.27

Health Care Index: 73.25

Visa requirement for US citizens: No visa required for 3 months

Visa requirement for UK citizens: No visa required for 3 months

Visa requirement for Israel citizens: No visa required for 3 months

I've been to this country before for reasons beyond sandboarding, as my family used to live here before they moved back to the U.K. very recently, I was very close to sandboarding here once, but sadly plans had to change, much to my disappointment. The best place to sandboard here in Germany was covered in a YouTube video by viral legend Tom Scott. Named "Monte Kaolino", the man-made hill "*is made from 35 million tons of quartz sand that was a biproduct of a nearby mine.*" (Lorelli, M. 2022) Every so often, the kaolinite has to be transported back to the top of the dune, and these carriers also take adventurers to the top to ski and sandboard down the dune; a one-way trip to the top takes no more than 2 minutes.

"Sandski Mont Kaolino" by Skinarr is licensed under CC BY-SA 4.0.

Greece

Crime Rate: 47.41

Cost of Living Index: 56.22

Quality of Life Index: 129.24

Health Care Index: 57.31

Visa requirement for US citizens: No visa required for 3 months

Visa requirement for UK citizens: No visa required for 3 months

Visa requirement for Israel citizens: No visa required for 3 months

On the Greek island of Lemnos, a unique landscape appears to be arid and dry compared to the rest of the country. Situated in the Aegean Sea, sandwiched between the mainlands of Greece and Turkiye, the island of Lemnos is home to a small so-called 'desert' called Gomati that's around 17 acres in area. "*The sand dunes, also known as "Pachies Ammoudies," are one of the most unique attractions on the island Lemnos, created by natural erosion caused by the prevailing winds blowing from across the sea.*" (Zikakou, I. 2021) Many filmmakers are known to come here to shoot scenes to replicate the desert or to imitate the Sahara, added with the iconic

Aegean Sea nearby; I would suspect that the vistas alone would be worth a visit.

"Αμμοθηνες" by Sotiriskostoulas is licensed under CC BY-SA 4.0.

Ireland

Crime Rate: 45.48

Cost of Living Index: 76.05

Quality of Life Index: 154.52

Health Care Index: 52.34

Visa requirement for US citizens: No visa required for 3 months

Visa requirement for UK citizens: No visa required (Common Travel Area)

Visa requirement for Israel citizens: No visa required for 3 months

Thanks for this dune discovery to the one and only Dr Dune of Sand Master Park back in Oregon. The Dunes of Curracloe near Wexford is on a stunning stretch of Irish coastline that is 11 kilometres long and is a clean place to relax, from what I'm told. In a poll by the Irish Independent, it was rated the Top beach in Ireland; Curracloe has its own surf shack, which offers Sandboarding classes and board hire; readers of the Irish Independent said the following about Curracloe Beach. *"No competition here, nothing but sand; it stretches for miles with a lovely forest trail beside it."* (Ó Conghaile, P. 2022). On the road, the dunes are 2 hours from Dublin.

Still, in my view, I'd hire a car as public transport will often just take you to Wexford, and you'll have a long walk from some of the nearest bus stops.

"Curracloe Beach White Gap 2012 10 01" by Andreas F. Borchert is licensed under CC BY-SA 3.0.

Italy

Crime Rate: 45.2

Cost of Living Index: 66.47

Quality of Life Index: 141.07

Health Care Index: 66.79

Visa requirement for US citizens: No visa required for 3 months

Visa requirement for UK citizens: No visa required for 3 months

Visa requirement for Israel citizens: No visa required for 3 months

You would think that European laws would dictate that some things would just be off-limits, but what if I told you that you could use a volcano board down Mount Etna. To my surprise, Mount Etna is a hub for those looking for adventure; you're free to mountain bike, hike, paraglide, and explore caves around and on Mount Etna, as well as go down on a sandboard. You need to be aware, as with any volcano, that rules could change at a moment's notice, and if it looks unsafe, don't do it, especially slide down on a sandboard. If you want the harsh facts: "*Mt Etna has killed 77 people in its history. This may sound like a lot, but the last serious incident was in 1979 when 9 people died during a hike to the summit crater. As a result, you now have to have a guide with you to hike up to this crater."* (Wright, R. 2021) You're free to take a hike or extreme volcano boarding, but if you're planning on doing this and not taking the cable car, you are obligated to have a guide.

"Mount Etna on Sicily in Italy - 2016-10-08 E" by Vicky Brock is licensed under CC BY-SA 2.0.

Poland

Crime Rate: 29.79

Cost of Living Index: 38.95

Quality of Life Index: 140.02

Health Care Index: 57.76

Visa requirement for US citizens: No visa required for 3 months

Visa requirement for UK citizens: No visa required for 3 months

Visa requirement for Israel citizens: No visa required for 3 months

Just like Albania and Denmark, I had no consideration. Instead, I thought of Poland when deciding where my Top 100 Sand dunes would be. Still, after I looked up the Łeba dunes at the Słowinski National Park, I was immediately intrigued and guessed it would have been near Kaliningrad. Kaliningrad is home to inaccessible dunes on the Curonian Spit; instead, these dunes are in the northern area of Poland. "*Unique in all of Europe and remarkable for their persistence and height, these coastal mountains are surrounded by ocean on one side with dune-locked lakes and forests on the other. But the 40 meter (131 feet) tall dunes are slowly overtaking the trees and where once tall, proud pines held sway, only fossilized tips poke out of the top of the mounds now."* (Atlas Obscura, 2016) Although these dunes are part of a national park, they aren't given special protection. Despite their constant shift throughout the years, there hasn't been any political will to prevent adventurers from venturing onto these mounds.

"Leba Dunes" by Medicaster40 is a public domain work.

Portugal

Crime Rate: 30.58

Cost of Living Index: 47.94

Quality of Life Index: 162.52

Health Care Index: 71.97

Visa requirement for US citizens: No visa required for 3 months

Visa requirement for UK citizens: No visa required for 3 months

Visa requirement for Israel citizens: No visa required for 3 months

Before the last book's publication, I didn't think there were sandboarding-worthy dunes in Portugal. The Salir Do Porto dunes aren't too far from Lisbon and Porto; they are regularly maintained, cleaned, and all well kept in a good state for the flocks of tourists that visit the beaches. "*Currently, the Salir dune is considered the largest in Portugal. However, it is said that it was once the largest on the European continent.*" (Santos Sousa, F. 2022) It sure sounds believable that Salir Do Porto could have historically been the highest dune on the continent; it's known that the tallest is the Dune of Pilat in France. Considering that there are many nearby facilities, including shops, restaurants, hotels, and toilets for nearby tourists, I'd undoubtedly go here if, for any reason, I couldn't visit the Dune du Pilat. I've never been to Portugal yet, but looking at this dune makes me want to see it.

"Duna de Salir do Porto (Portugal) (22161468)" by Vitor Oliveira is licensed under CC BY-SA 2.0.

Russia

Crime Rate: 39.62

Cost of Living Index: 35.26 (lowest in Europe)

Quality of Life Index: 103.28 (lowest in Europe)

Health Care Index: 59.08

Visa requirement for US citizens: Visa required

Visa requirement for UK citizens: Visa required

Visa requirement for Israel citizens: No visa required for 3 months

Wars and conflicts aside, it's no surprise that the world's largest country would be bound to have something going for it when it comes to a Sandboarding presence; this is mainly down to a few and far between dune regions in the entire country. Unlike shifting sands and beaches that would otherwise naturally have dunes that pop up from nowhere, the dunes of Sychevo are something that doesn't conform to a stereotype of Russian land as this was the doing of a quarry. "*If you search for unusual landscape, which is not typical for Central Russia, 100 km from Moscow, there is such an exotic place. This is a sand quarry in Sychevo, a vast territory about 8 km long with* dunes and small lakes, thickets of sea buckthorn and excavators. The way to get here is not easy to find, so it is not a crowded place. Some people come here for extreme sports, some come to relax on a sandy beach, but many come just to see this peculiar Moscow-area desert." (Derzhavina, V. 2019)

"Карьер около Сычево - panoramio" by citrin is licensed under CC BY-SA 3.0.

Spain

Crime Rate: 33.87

Cost of Living Index: 53.88

Quality of Life Index: 168.48

Health Care Index: 78.37

Visa requirement for US citizens: No visa required for 3 months

Visa requirement for UK citizens: No visa required for 3 months

Visa requirement for Israel citizens: No visa required for 3 months

In my occupation, I am well aware that every Brit that's gone abroad on holiday has most certainly visited Spain once in their life, but this sport is most likely not the reason. This first place of three is the only one on the mainland; the other two will be based in the Canary Islands. Not far from Gibraltar is the town of Tarifa and this town is home to the nearby Duna de Bolonia; it's no small region either; it's easily one of the more extended dune regions in Spain, if not Europe. "*Four kilometers long, it is a spectacular sandy beach full of dunes where you can enjoy the sun, the sea breeze and its waters, and on clear days you can see Africa perfectly on the horizon."* (Uppers, 2022)

"Bolonia (1981) 06" by LBM1948 is licensed under CC BY-SA 4.0.

And now, onto a place I have gladly mentioned before, Maspalomas in the Canary Islands, is known to be a trendy destination for hitting sand dunes in Spain. There is a sandboarding school, and camels can be ridden across the dunes for a price. However, there is a protected area of the dunes, which is off-limits, so as long as you steer clear of that zone, I am assured you will have a great session on the dunes.

"Dunas de Maspalomas, Gran Canaria" by Marcela Střelcová is licensed under CC BY-SA 4.0.

From Gran Canaria to Fuerteventura, not much is known about the Dunes of Corralejo, which don't sit too far from the blue water beach on the Northwestern portion of Fuerteventura. This area and the neighbouring Lobos Island were declared a natural park and reserve until the 1980s. The dunes are: "*Varied and unspoilt, they are perfect for water sports and are nudist friendly. If Fuerteventura is that 'piece of Saharan Africa lost in the Atlantic'—as the Basque philosopher Miguel de*

Unamuno referred to it—then Corralejo sand dunes no doubt represent the beating heart of that African desert." (Barceló Experiences, n.d.) A final note on these dunes: they are described as nudist-friendly; if it's not to your taste, you have been warned.

"Matas, Dunas de Corralejo, Fuerteventura, España, 2015" by Benjamín Núñez González is licensed under CC BY-SA 4.0.

United Kingdom

Crime Rate: 46.47

Cost of Living Index: 69.65

Quality of Life Index: 161.74

Health Care Index: 74.83

Visa requirement for US citizens: No visa required for 6 months

Visa requirement for UK citizens: None, because you're British.

Visa requirement for Israel citizens: No visa required for 6 months

I'm on home territory, so I should be the least biased regarding dunes in the United Kingdom; the first ones I'll have to mention are the dunes I was introduced to the sport and, quite frankly, shaped me today. Holywell is a small village not too far from the A3075 road and around 15 minutes from Newquay, home of another great event, the Boardmasters Surf Festival. As for facilities for learning how to Sandboard, the UK as a whole is lacking, and if I'm honest, Ireland does it better than we do, but that's not to say the UK hasn't got people sandboarding, because I am one of those people.

"Holywell bay tallest dune view from apex towards sea 20150812" by Jack Soley is licensed under CC BY 3.0.

The next prominent place in England isn't too far from Cornwall; one county over in Devon, the dunes in Braunton Burrows are home to a specific athlete, Alex Bird. If you recall from my last book, you'll know him as the man who broke the UK land speed record on a sandboard. As you may also know, where there's sand, there's surf. To make Cornwall a bit jealous, North Devon recently became the first place in the UK selected as a World Surfing Reserve. To put it bluntly from a BBC article: "*And an area around Braunton Burrows is a Unesco Biosphere for its landscapes, wildlife areas and cultural heritage. The reserve covers about 30km (19 miles) of coastline. A WSR spokesperson said: "Its high density of outstanding surf, at iconic breaks such as Croyde, Saunton, Woolacombe, and Lynmouth, caters to wave-riders from beginner to expert and a variety of surfing styles.""* (BBC, 2022)

"Army training manoeuvres on Braunton Burrows - geograph.org.uk - 404510" by Thor Beverley is licensed under CC BY-SA 2.0.

Elsewhere in the United Kingdom, another dune that I know well is near the town of Bridgend in South Wales; the village is Merthyr Mawr, and the dune is "Big Dipper" and has been recognised to be the 2nd highest in Europe. It's also been recorded that "*The dunes at Merthyr Mawr were used during the filming of Lawrence of Arabia*" (Nation.Cymru, 2022) and given the landscape, it would be easy to see why. In addition, the dunes nowadays are used for training for Rugby players as the high climb and vertical slope makes it perfect for fast, uphill running; since this is the closest dune to my house, don't be shocked if we meet here.

"Sand dunes at Merthyr Mawr Warren - geograph.org.uk - 2551881" by Nick Smith is licensed under CC BY-SA 2.0.

Finally, you might have noticed on this UK list I have unknowingly travelled from the south to the north, as the final destination for the United Kingdom, and indeed the European section of this book is the Balmedie dunes of Scotland. This section of Aberdeenshire is a stone's throw away from a golf resort owned by none other than former U.S. president Donald Trump. "*At Balmedie Beach, you'll have glistening water in front of you and picturesque sand dunes and grassland behind you. Balmedie Country*

Park has 1700 metres of boardwalk to help you explore the dunes and soak up the views." (The Press and Journal, 2022)

"Balmedie Dunes - geograph.org.uk - 322394" by Colin Galloway is licensed under CC BY-SA 2.0.

Asia

This continent is home to the most people, and it's home to a large proportion of the world's land area & population. Some of the countries that are included here are some I've yet to even mention on my blog because there's a statistic such as low living standards or how hard it is to get a visa, or simply because I made a Top 10 list, there were 10 countries better than them. Before I dive into this list, the sandboarding here isn't just on the Arabian Peninsula. Asia is home to many countries, and these countries have a lot of potential for keen athletes.

(People's Republic of) China

Crime Rate: 29.39

Cost of Living Index: 41.77

Quality of Life Index: 105.07

Health Care Index: 66.4

Visa requirement for US citizens: Visa required

Visa requirement for UK citizens: Visa required

Visa requirement for Israel citizens: Visa required

It would only be natural to assume that one of the world's most influential countries would have something in terms of sand dunes, and I would bet every pound I have on there being a sandboarding scene in China. I discovered some of the undiscovered and unknown Chinese Sandboarding in the last book, where I spoke about Mingsha Mountain, also known as the Singing Sand Dunes (not to be confused with the ones in Qatar, but I'll get to them later). The dunes are a hotspot for camel riding and, no surprise, Sandboarding. According to Chinese state media reported by CNN: "*Visitors to the Mingsha Mountain and Crescent Spring will now be safe from camel collisions, thanks to the new traffic signal, which turns green to let the animals cross and red to make them stop."* (Guy, J. 2021) That's right, there are traffic crossings for camels around the dune. If the sandboarding ramps up here, those signals could become very useful.

"鸣沙山" by Yanxutong1215 is licensed under CC BY-SA 4.0.

Head due east from Mingsha Mountain. You'll be in a desert for a long while, but after the desert and mountains, another fantastic destination for hitting the dunes is Shapotou in the Ningxia Hui autonomous region; this area is relatively new and, at the time of writing, has a newly built library in the desert, a first in China. "*With flowing dunes stretching spectacularly into the distance, the three-story, abstractionist-style library opened in June in the city of Zhongwei and is an architectural success, according to Jin Weiqi, a Beijing-based photographer. The chocolate color building looks like an inclined box half-buried in the desert. Using rusty iron sheets on its exterior to keep out desert heat, the "Lost Treasure Box" library seems like a boat stranded on a beach.*" (Xinhua, 2022) This dune area is situated within a region known as the Tengger Desert; Sandboarding, camel riding, bungee jumping, and zip-wiring across the Yellow River are a few activities that can be done here.

"Shapotou desert area (20171005173240)" by N509FZ is licensed under CC BY-SA 4.0.

Since I started writing about China in this book, I've felt really optimistic and interested in these places; the final destination for Sandboarding I'd include in China is the Tianmo Sand Sliding Field which is under 100km from Beijing. When the words "Sand Sliding" are in the place's name, you're onto a winner. It's a haven for sportspeople and film buffs: "*People can not only go sand sliding, sand hill climbing and camel riding, but they may also have a chance to watch the shooting of movie and television scenes. Because of its unique landscape, Tianmo Sand Sliding Field has become one of the best locations to shoot pictures of the scenery of western China. In recent years, more than 300 films and TV series chose this place as a filming location, examples are: The Romance of The Three Kingdoms, and A Pilgrimage to The West."* (Pang, K. 2021) Without any noise of the big city, no industrial background atmosphere, an abundance of peace and quiet will be your expectation for this place.

Unfortunately, I couldn't find a free-to-use image of the dunes, but I have sourced a satellite image that'll give a rough indication of the location; it's in the centre-right!

"Sanggan River confluence in Yanghe River IMG 4155 Huailai and Zhuolu counties, Zhangjiakou, Hebei" by Bjoertvedt is licensed under CC BY-SA 4.0.

India

Crime Rate: 44.63

Cost of Living Index: 24.43

Quality of Life Index: 110.99

Health Care Index: 65.66

Visa requirement for US citizens: E-visa valid for 6 months

Visa requirement for UK citizens: Visa required

Visa requirement for Israel citizens: E-visa valid for 2 months

I once was a tourist in India, not for sports or anything close, but with one of my best friends to visit family, and I can say that India is not only a beautiful country. Unbeknown to me, it's also home to a small desert, good enough for a Sandboarding scene to develop. This part of India is undoubtedly presented to be luxurious and awash with places to stay that will give you a pleasant, warm feeling. "*The royal dessert city of India also known as the golden city, Jaisalmer's charm lies in the grandeur and glory of its forts and palaces. With the massive sand dunes on one hand and the colourful bazaars on the other, this trip will fill you with rich cultural heritage.*

The visit to the wondrous Thar desert along with exciting adventure sports, desert safaris, and delectable cuisines will keep you going!' (Daijiworld, 2022)

"Thar desert Rajasthan India" by sushmita balasubramani is licensed under CC BY 2.0.

Indonesia

Crime Rate: 46.12

Cost of Living Index: 35.85

Quality of Life Index: 90.36

Health Care Index: 60.44

Visa requirement for US citizens: No visa required for 1 month

Visa requirement for UK citizens: No visa required for 1 month

Visa requirement for Israel citizens: Visa required

If you asked me to name some dunes in Indonesia this time last year, I wouldn't have been able to give you an answer; but now I have been introduced to the charms of the Parangkusumo dunes, within a scenic sandy area known as "Gumuk Pasir". I haven't included any references to these dunes because one source mentioned that there aren't a lot of sand dunes in the world (hint: I'm naming at least a hundred here!) and the other said that there were only 2 sand dunes in the world, the other being in Mexico. The dunes of Parangkusumo lie in the Central South of Java. If you want to get here from Jakarta, it'll be 9 hours by car, but if you arrive from

Yogyakarta International Airport, the dunes are only 40km away. Many sources have mentioned the potential for Sandboarding, and it's one of the everyday activities here, and with Java's high population, I see no reason why Sandboarding doesn't explode here… If not, there's always the chance of volcano boarding at a nearby summit.

"Sandboarding di Gumuk Pasir Parangtritis" by Hendrojkson is licensed under CC BY-SA 4.0.

Iran

Crime Rate: 49.11

Cost of Living Index: 37.39

Quality of Life Index: 64.89 (lowest in Asia)

Health Care Index: 52.3 (lowest in Asia)

Visa requirement for US citizens: Visa required

Visa requirement for UK citizens: Visa required

Visa requirement for Israel citizens: Admission refused

Stereotypically, Iran hasn't been very western friendly since the late 1970s; however, that doesn't mean that the people aren't friendly, which couldn't be further from the truth, according to what I've heard from many Iranians. It may have a large portion of rocky mountains and desert, and its features like these make Iran a good place for Sandboarding. However, poor quality of life and declining living standards make an excellent case for Iranians to leave the country. Still, there are some incredible locations for those staying in and those who live elsewhere and want to sandboard here. Near Isfahan, Iran's 3rd largest city, is the Varzaneh Desert, a habitat for the earth and water-bound animals. As for the deserts' opportunities: "*Sand therapy, walking on the sand dunes, cycling, riding an all-terrain vehicle (ATVs), off-roading, skiing on the sand and camel trekking are the tourism capacities of the desert. The beauty of the desert is tied to its boundless calmness and the silence that surrounds all the depths of human existence.*" (Tasnim News Agency, 2019)

"Photographying in Varzaneh desert, Varzaneh, Isfahan" by Mohammadjavad Ebrahimi is licensed under CC BY-SA 4.0.

Staying in the central provinces of Iran, but going east a little the Rig-E Zarin desert also known as the Golden Desert or the Moghestan Desert is a remarkable jewel in the Iranian crown as this desert is a lot less visited than the other regions of the country. In the hot seasons, the temperatures exceed what would be deemed habitable for the average human. Quite scarily, this desert isn't signposted for tourists or has a lot of facilities, so if you like nothing but the sound of your voice, this might be the spot for you, one article writes. "*The Rig-e Zarin has fewer visitors than many other well-known deserts such as the Marnjab and Mesr, and therefore its tranquility and silence is remarkable, especially during the night. Of course, this factor can create dangers for tourists. Because in most parts of the desert there are no signs for guidance, the chances of getting lost are high.*" (Gholami, M. 2020) So if you fancy getting out of this desert, follow your footprints; but the tranquility and mystery make this sandboarding spot worthy of being on this list. I couldn't find free images of this specific location, so I've included something within the Yazd Province, where Rig-E Zarin is located.

"Kavire yazd (2)" by Fariba.tavakkoli is licensed under CC BY-SA 4.0.

Israel

Crime Rate: 32.12

Cost of Living Index: 88.05 (highest in this book)

Quality of Life Index: 146.06

Health Care Index: 73.83

Visa requirement for US citizens: No visa required for 3 months

Visa requirement for UK citizens: No visa required for 3 months

Visa requirement for Israel citizens: None, because you're Israeli.

Regarding my blog, Israel was the 3rd most popular country for readership. I was aware that Israeli citizens would also have difficulty entering certain countries. I am sure to get schtick for this; From what I have witnessed, Israel is a technologically and politically progressive country compared to some of its foes in the region. Many people will have differing opinions on this country's legitimacy. Still, no matter where you are on the Israel-Palestine conflict, you cannot dispute that the land is some of the most historically significant and holds beautiful grounds in the Levant. Sandboarding is a big thing here; tour agencies and companies will happily take you on a journey into the Negev Desert. Still, I'd recommend the dunes surrounding the city of Ashdod, as it's not too far from the coast and roughly halfway between Tel Aviv and the Gaza Strip. If you're looking to visit, be aware this is one of the last coastal sand dunes in Israel, and the city of Ashdod wishes to expand with housing and education; there are efforts to keep these dunes as a nature preserve. Only time will tell if the dunes remain, and I hope they do.

"Duna velki 024" by Ori~ is licensed under CC BY-SA 3.0.

Japan

Crime Rate: 22.12

Cost of Living Index: 77.03

Quality of Life Index: 169.48 (highest in Asia)

Health Care Index: 80.49

Visa requirement for US citizens: No visa required for 3 months

Visa requirement for UK citizens: No visa required for 6 months

Visa requirement for Israel citizens: No visa required for 3 months

Japan is a highly cultural country. Japan has many reasons to visit, for the volume of shrines and gardens or the buzz of the big cities of Tokyo and Osaka. For example, people come here for skiing in the winter, and they also visit Tottori when they're not skiing. Nearby is a sand museum, so if you get tired of the dunes, you can always see some sand-related creations. It should be known that writing messages in the dunes is illegal, and the local government is doing everything in its power to prevent it. These dunes are ancient and it sounds hypocritical how board sports are allowed but writing isn't. The authorities are doing everything to avoid graffiti being put on the dunes, "*Officials have added signs in English, Chinese, and Korean to make sure all visitors know the rules.*" (Christofaro, B. 2019)

"Tottori sand dune p1 2600" by 663highland is licensed under CC BY-SA 3.0.

Jordan

Crime Rate: 40.24

Cost of Living Index: 49.19

Quality of Life Index: 113.92

Health Care Index: 65.57

Visa requirement for US citizens: Visa on arrival for 1 month

Visa requirement for UK citizens: Visa on arrival

Visa requirement for Israel citizens: No visa required

Jordan is a kingdom in the middle of Israel and Saudi Arabia; it's probably most well known as the host of the ancient city of Petra. On the same highway as Petra, you can reach the Wadi Rum, an area of the desert well-known for Sandboarding. Wadi Rum is within a protected area known as the Valley of the Moon, as well as surfing down sand dunes, there are many things to discover when you're in this specific area of Jordan, one reporter for The Times who documented their journey of the King's Highway put it well: "*we drove into the Khazali Canyon to see 2,000-year-old inscriptions about camels etched by the Thamud, an ancient Arab tribe; we visited the rubble-remains of Lawrence of Arabia's house; we sand-boarded down flame-red dunes; and rode a camel back to camp. It was fun, but felt as though it was an itinerary for more impatient tourists."* (Bakht, S. 2022) Jordan may not be a big country, but just like Israel next door, it's no argument that this holds some of the world's most diverse and historically significant lands.

"Wadi Rum Protected Area, Jordan" by Alessandro Balsamo is licensed under CC BY-SA 3.0.

Kazakhstan

Crime Rate: 53.45

Cost of Living Index: 28.68

Quality of Life Index: 93.77

Health Care Index: 59.99

Visa requirement for US citizens: No visa required for 1 month

Visa requirement for UK citizens: No visa required for 1 month

Visa requirement for Israel citizens: No visa required for 1 month

I will be honest, I would imagine a lot of people would assume that this place is known because of a particular motion picture by Sacha Baron Cohen, but Borat aside, Kazakhstan is not only one of the largest countries in the world by land area, it also plays home to the Altyn-Emel National Park; a project manager of the Kazakh National Geographic Society said in the following in an article: "*There are eco-toilets, gazebos for rest, grottos (special shade awnings), drinking fountains, where tourists can quench their thirst, as well as observation decks. The same tourist facilities will be ensured in the Altyn Emel area and, for now, there is an observation tower, from which animals can be observed. There will be more towers installed later*" (Bulatkulova, S. 2021). So it's clear that Kazakhstan is on a mission to drum up tourist opportunities for the country; however, if you're wondering where the Sandboarding comes into this park, it has a "Singing Sand Dune" that's open to adventure seekers, which has a height of 150 metres.

"Altyn Emel 2020 10" by Sane4o is licensed under CC BY-SA 4.0.

Malaysia

Crime Rate: 55.71 (highest in Asia)

Cost of Living Index: 37.02

Quality of Life Index: 117.98

Health Care Index: 70.14

Visa requirement for US citizens: No visa required for 3 months

Visa requirement for UK citizens: No visa required for 3 months

Visa requirement for Israel citizens: Visa required

Here's a country with a lot of cultural influence in South East Asia; Malaysia is known for a few sports; one that comes to mind is Formula One when it hosts the Malaysian Grand Prix. Another is known because I've had some interest in seeing it played, Sepak Takraw, which is a bit like volleyball but involves kicking. Sandboarding isn't a sport you'd typically associate with Malaysia. But there are some beaches in the country where you can take part in this pastime. One of the best spots is the Malacca Sand Dunes, which is often confused with Klebang within this area. They're not particularly tall dunes and aren't natural formations but man-made sand mounds from a failed land reclamation project. For helpful directions to the dunes: "*Once you're at the car park, continue on foot for 1.6 kilometers until you hit the sand dunes. This is the minimum distance you need to walk, one-way. Crossing the pipe can be difficult for those with walking difficulties. There is a spot where they made a little ramp to get motorcycles across. This ramp isn't wide enough for a wheelchair. The path beyond the pipe isn't too sandy for wheels right until the low-relief sand dunes at the start. One could also bike the distance beyond the pipe.*" (Veldwijk, I. 2020)

Unfortunately, there are no free images of these dunes available but this is the nearby beach before you reach the dunes:

"Klebang Beach" by Chongkian is licensed under CC BY-SA 4.0.

Mongolia

Crime Rate: 53.73

Cost of Living Index: 34.74

Quality of Life Index: Not Known

Health Care Index: Not Known

Visa requirement for US citizens: No visa required for 3 months

Visa requirement for UK citizens: Visa required

Visa requirement for Israel citizens: No visa required for 1 month

Mongolia will always be known for its Empire and today's modern state is nowhere near the size and influence of its predecessor; the Gobi Desert is found in a large part of Mongolia, and naturally sand dunes are found in this desert. There's not a lot of people and the population density is absurdly low, Mongolia even holds the Guinness World Record for 'Most Sparsely Populated Country'; statistics aside, the most notable sand dune site in this country sits within Mongolia's largest national park: Gobi Gurvansaikhan. *It's located in the northern part of the Gobi and is home to the Gurvan Saikhan Mountains, hence its name. The park is famous for the dunes of Khongoryn Els, nicknamed the Singing Sands, because of the sound it makes during strong winds."* (Bhatia, A. 2022) Looking at images, I've been lost looking at the landscape of this nation and given the fact it has such a low population density, it's good if you want to get away from people. If you like the sound of being secluded, at peace, and having more dunes than people; Khongoryn Els is the place for you.

"Khongoryn Els, Gurvansaikhan NP, Gobi desert, Mongolia" by Severin.stalder is licensed under CC BY-SA 3.0.

Oman

Crime Rate: 19.99

Cost of Living Index: 49.42

Quality of Life Index: 173.68 (highest in Asia)

Health Care Index: 58.23

Visa requirement for US citizens: E-visa valid for 1 week

Visa requirement for UK citizens: E-visa valid for 1 month

Visa requirement for Israel citizens: Visa required

Naturally, a country that holds a large part of desert will indeed have sand dunes within them for sandboarding purposes. Every trip to Oman will be complete with a visit to the desert. You'll be amazed that there are many opportunities for you to stay in traditional Bedouin style with a fire in the sands, the chance to eat many locally produced foods and stargazing at the night sky. The wind sculpted dunes of the Sharqiya Sands (also known as the Wahiba Sands) provide this perfect experience. These sands feed into the Empty Quarter which primarily lies in Saudi Arabia. A good description of your arrival can be summarised quite nicely: "*you're surrounded by undulating dunes and desert vegetation in a seemingly infinite landscape that feels like it was crafted out of gold when the sun is low in the sky. These wind-sculpted dunes, some as high as 100m (328ft), continue on into the famous Empty Quarter, one of the largest sand deserts in the world."* (Amar, N. 2022) These dunes lie primarily empty and there are the brave few who cross these sands in off-road vehicles, the more courageous few who cross on camels, and the most courageous cross on sandboards.

"Wahiba Sands 07" by albinfo is licensed under CC BY-SA 4.0.

Pakistan

Crime Rate: 42.01

Cost of Living Index: 19.92 (lowest in this book)

Quality of Life Index: 102.57

Health Care Index: 59.58

Visa requirement for US citizens: E-visa required

Visa requirement for UK citizens: E-visa required

Visa requirement for Israel citizens: Admission refused

In general, when a lot of people think about Pakistan, an image is presented as a hot and mountainous desert country; however where we're off to is not just one of the world's highest deserts, the temperature here can drop as low as -25C (-13F) but in the summers can feel relatively calm compared to the rest of the country. The Katpana Desert (also known as the Cold Desert) lies in the high north of Pakistan not far from India's contested border. It's also within the Karakorams, a mountain range home to the world's second highest mountain, K2; this mountain range lies in this area of oddly placed sand dunes. The British Backpacker Society described Pakistan as one of the friendliest countries on earth, and it's easy to see why when you look at the stunning scenery this country offers. The best times to visit this desert are in the daytime between June & September and the desert itself less than 10 kilometres from the airport, if you were mad enough to do this trip in a day… you could.

"Sakardu Pakistan by Aref Majeed 3" by Arefmajeed is licensed under CC BY-SA 4.0.

Philippines

Crime Rate: 42.33

Cost of Living Index: 37.06

Quality of Life Index: 83.74

Health Care Index: 67.53

Visa requirement for US citizens: No visa required for 1 month

Visa requirement for UK citizens: No visa required for 1 month

Visa requirement for Israel citizens: No visa required for 2 months

The Philippines are known for many natural wonders on its many islands, so it was just going to happen that sand dunes would appear on at least one of its 2,000 inhabited islands. The dunes of Paoay on the north-west of Luzon Island. These dunes are popular with tourists inside and outside the country; the whole site is just under 100 square kilometres and is a big hit with 4x4 enthusiasts. "In pre-pandemic times, the Paoay sand dunes have been a popular filming destination for local and international production companies. It is also a favorite among thrill-seekers eager to try dune-bashing, sand boarding, and 4x4 activities." (Adriano, L. 2022) An annual festival called the "Himala sa Buhangin" is held here with many contemporary art installations which in turn also draw people here for purposes other than sport; this makes the province of Ilocos Norte and the Paoay dunes a very desirable hotspot for travellers; "*As the first and only province to receive a safe travel stamp from the World Travel and Tourism Council, Ilocos Norte continues to promote new normal attractions in various parts of the province to entice more tourists and generate more jobs for the locals.*" (Adriano, L. 2022)

"Paoay sand dunes" by Froirivera is licensed under CC BY-SA 4.0.

Qatar

Crime Rate: 13.78 (lowest in this book)

Cost of Living Index: 62.81

Quality of Life Index: 154.53

Health Care Index: 73.53

Visa requirement for US citizens: No visa required for 1 month

Visa requirement for UK citizens: No visa required for 1 month

Visa requirement for Israel citizens: Visa required

This country came onto the map for many people because of its somewhat controversial hosting of the 2022 FIFA World Cup, but football tournaments to one side; for adventure seekers and adrenaline addicts, Qatar has many sports on land, sea, and air to offer. This little peninsula bordering Saudi Arabia hosts a sand dune complex, one of the many "Singing Sand Dunes" in Asia. Between Al-Wakrah and Mesaieed you will find these sand dunes that sing, groan, creak, or any noise you might appropriately describe. But you might be asking, what makes these singing dunes different? Well, when you're on the sands overlooking this tiny state; *Riders can traverse dunes against the blue backdrop of the Inland Sea, a UNESCO world heritage site."* (Thompson, N. 2022) But due to this country's immense wealth, if you want to go skydiving, deep sea diving, dune bashing, visiting museums, exploring ancient history, why not do it all in Qatar?

"Singing sand dunes" by Peter Dowley is licensed under CC BY 2.0.

Taiwan (Republic of China)

Crime Rate: 15.87

Cost of Living Index: 62.35

Quality of Life Index: 140.15

Health Care Index: 86.43 (highest in this book)

Visa requirement for US citizens: No visa required for 3 months

Visa requirement for UK citizens: No visa required

Visa requirement for Israel citizens: No visa required

Before I begin my piece on this particular country, I am fully aware of the dispute between PRC and the ROC in international relations, however I am treating these two entities as separate territories in this book even though I acknowledge that many organisations and establishments have a differing opinion. The city of Taipei which is the capital is in the North of the island, but if you go to near the island's southernmost point, you can find the Jiupeng desert where you can find a small sand dune region where many off road vehicles love to test their equipment. The nearby dunes include Gangzai which are such a trivial distance apart they may as well be included in the same dune complex. Closer to Taipei, the Taoyuan dunes are an hours' drive from the capital and have fencing and a footpath to guide tourists along the sands. I've decided to include the Jiupeng Desert in my official list as there is a small list of sandboarding areas within Taiwan. Furthermore, it needs to be clearly defined if sports are allowed in Taoyuan where it's tolerated in Jiupeng; and the dunes in Jiupeng are much higher.

"九棚沙漠 *Jiupeng Coastal Dunes - panoramio" by Lienyuan Lee is licensed under CC BY 3.0.*

Türkiye

Crime Rate: 39.69

Cost of Living Index: 28.31

Quality of Life Index: 124.05

Health Care Index: 70.83

Visa requirement for US citizens: E-visa valid for 3 months

Visa requirement for UK citizens: No visa required for 3 months

Visa requirement for Israel citizens: No visa required for 3 months

Two things: Firstly, I've placed this country in the Asia section as both of these places are outside of Eastern Thrace so I don't consider them the European part of the country, I'm sorry; Secondly in 2022, the Turkish government made an official request to change the country's English name from "Turkey" to "Türkiye" so I apologise if it threw you off slightly. Türkiye is a top-rated holiday destination for those who think Spain is too monotonous and fancy somewhere different. This country has coasts on the Mediterranean and Black Seas and isn't lacking of sandy shores no matter which of these coastlines you choose; when it comes to Sandboarding in the country, Antalya is one of the country's largest cities and is a giant tourist hotspot, "*Patara Beach on Turkey's Mediterranean coast is drawing great interest from tourists for its sand dunes that have provided opportunities for local tourism operators to launch horse and camel tours.*" (Hürriyet Daily News, 2017) The beach with the dunes is 18 kilometres in length and there is a small fee of under 10 Lira for access to the beach, Sandboarding is most definitely practised here however if you come here, you'll find more people on horses than boards.

"Sand Dunes of Patara" by Begüm Berik is licensed under CC BY-SA 4.0.

When it comes to this sport, you have to go near a beach or venture to an inland desert, Karapinar in Central Anatolia is the second best sandboarding spot in Türkiye but it wasn't always this way… Wind erosion and the lack of precipitation made the dunes form along with a desert-like landscape in the 1960s, around a quarter of a million acres of land was turned into dry land and crop yields decreased dramatically. The location is a fair distance from the coast and isn't far from a main highway, "*Located on the historic Silk Road, Karapınar attracts many visitors with its desert and tectonic lakes. This natural wonder desert is also one of the rare safari spots in Turkey.*" (TRT, 2022) The historical connections go back to around 2,000 BCE where a nearby volcanic field was formed; the sand is distinctly more rockier here but the desert in Central Anatolia makes a perfect sporting environment and a backdrop for a memorable journey.

"Karapınar 2010 Acıgöl-Maar" by Volker Höhfeld is licensed under CC BY-SA 4.0.

Vietnam

Crime Rate: 45.81

Cost of Living Index: 37.48

Quality of Life Index: 89.95

Health Care Index: 58.92

Visa requirement for US citizens: E-visa valid for 1 month

Visa requirement for UK citizens: No visa required for 2 weeks

Visa requirement for Israel citizens: Visa required

Vietnam is becoming an ever increasing desirable location for leisure and adventure tourists, the many reasons this country is visited is because of its mass population of motorbike riders, trains that pass unfathomably close to houses, Ha Long Bay, and exhibitions from the time of the Vietnam War; these are all reasons why I would like to visit the country, a reason people wouldn't usually visit is for Sandboarding. The dunes of Mui Ne are only a 4 hour drive from Ho Chi Minh City and are littered with many people looking for perfect photos, and many companies that would naturally take you on the dunes in an all terrain vehicle or sandboard. As with many beach resorts in hot climates, visit when the sun isn't most prominent. "*Visiting the dunes in the late afternoon meant it was not too hot and the sand was comfortable to walk on. Strong winds might sweep the sand onto your bare skin or eyes, so wearing shades, hats and scarves would lessen the discomfort. My favourite part of the drive was definitely the ocean road drive towards the White Sand Dunes, a good 40 minutes away from the Mui Ne town. The vastness of the South China Sea, the sight of crashing waves and sprawling fields of greenery was a balm for the weary.*" (Tan, E.J. 2019)

"Vietnam, Mui Ne sand dunes" by Vyacheslav Argenberg is licensed under CC BY 4.0.

Yemen

Crime Rate: Not Known

Cost of Living Index: 53.14

Quality of Life Index: Not Known

Health Care Index: Not Known

Visa requirement for US citizens: Visa required

Visa requirement for UK citizens: Visa required

Visa requirement for Israel citizens: Admission refused

Yemen's Civil War has plagued the national image for a while on the international stage, it's not been in any stable state for a long time; many countries have discouraged its citizens from visiting the country and many states have closed its embassies. Conflict aside, Socotra Island which some may know from the Call of Duty game franchise, is an island in the Indian Ocean owned and administered by Yemen. Socotra's biodiversity is considered some of the best in the whole of Arabia, there are many dunes dotted across the island so I cannot possibly categorise each dune area individually because there's so many across the island. I can only gather little recent information because of the lack of demand, which comes from the ongoing civil war that unfortunately has spread to the island. Luckily, I have found a report on some of the isle's highest dunes at Arher Beach: "*Though they seem to be low gradient, one has to be capable of great endurance to climb the dunes – it is very difficult and wearisome to go up on loose sand. It will take you more than one hour to reach the top of the dunes. But doing that, you will be rewarded by breath-taking views on the Arabic sea and the Erissel Cape. You can also explore one of caves that more than enough here. Don't forget to take a couple of bottles with water.*" (Romanov, D. n.d.)

"Arher dunes (6408219309)" by Gerry & Bonni is licensed under CC BY 2.0.

Africa

This sport is unquestionably changing the lives of the people who live in Africa as adventure seekers and adrenaline junkies flock to visit the continent and take up Sandboarding as one of the many excursions that tour agencies have to offer. For the most part, the dunes will be present in the many deserts that call Africa their home but a small portion of these grand mounds of sand will be found on beaches and in sandy areas that otherwise wouldn't make sense if you looked at the location on a satellite map. This place also is a strong contender for where ancient Sandboarding was first discovered.

Algeria

Crime Rate: 53.82

Cost of Living Index: 26.87 (lowest in Africa)

Quality of Life Index: Not Known

Health Care Index: 52.88

Visa requirement for US citizens: Visa required

Visa requirement for UK citizens: Visa required

Visa requirement for Israel citizens: Admission refused

Algeria is currently the largest country on the African continent; that title was previously held by Sudan until South Sudan gained independence in 2011. Algeria is known for the Atlas Mountains and, just like a lot of North Africa, the Sahara Desert; going deeper, you'll find a lot of dune fields and Ergs in these North African countries. The dunes I will focus on for Algeria will be in and around the town of Tifernine which is a small town in Eastern Algeria, and is home to the dunes of that area, primarily quiet but considering the sheer size of the country, there really shouldn't be anywhere where Sandboarding isn't possible; speaking of Tifernine: "*This part of the Sahara Desert, located in eastern Algeria, abuts the dark grayish-brown Tinrhert Plateau. Winds have sculpted star dunes on top of older, larger dunes and evaporite minerals, including salt, have collected in small white depressions among the dunes. Today, the climate is arid and hot, but the river-carved valleys on the edge of the plateau give evidence of wetter times in the past."* (Mason, B. 2009) Given the size and height of the nearby Atlas Mountain range and the depth of colour from these copper dunes, it's almost as if you're not in Algeria but on Mars.

"ISS013-E-65515 - View of Algeria" by Earth Science and Remote Sensing Unit is a public domain work.

Botswana

Crime Rate: 52.37

Cost of Living Index: 40.17

Quality of Life Index: Not Known

Health Care Index: Not Known

Visa requirement for US citizens: No visa required for 3 months

Visa requirement for UK citizens: No visa required for 3 months

Visa requirement for Israel citizens: No visa required for 3 months

In a country I wouldn't consider having dunes but more safari adventures, this country pleasantly surprised me with having dunes in its borders. Botswana is home to the small village of Khawa in the Kgalagadi District, which doesn't boast much except for one time of the year where it hosts the Khawa Desert Challenge where quad bikes and motorbikes crash through the dunes around the area. Whenever vehicles aren't going in and around the dunes, this makes a perfect place to grab a Sandboard. As recently as 2022, the village has had significant improvements made to its infrastructure; "*Notably there were a lot of improvements within the village from the last Khawa event. Apart from receiving ten tents from the Ministry, Khawa village is now paved along the main road to the Kgotla and Government has also erected solar lights in most parts of the village, a great improvement to the village aesthetics and safety"* (Mathala, S. 2022)

"Border fence Namibia Botswana (2018)" by Hp.Baumeler is licensed under CC BY-SA 4.0.

Cabo Verde

Crime Rate: Not Known

Cost of Living Index: Not Known

Quality of Life Index: Not Known

Health Care Index: Not Known

Visa requirement for US citizens: No visa required for 1 month

Visa requirement for UK citizens: No visa required for 1 month

Visa requirement for Israel citizens: Visa on arrival

This country is a bunch of islands off the coast of West Africa, however these bunch of islands are home to the Viana Desert which is on the island of Boa Vista. Cabo Verde or Cape Verde to some, is a Portuguese-speaking country of around half a million inhabitants; when it comes to a good experience of visiting this desert, it sure will be a positive one! "*Boa Vista has its very own chunk of the Sahara; the grains of sand that make up the Viana desert are blown in from western Africa. Many tour operators offer dune buggy and quad-bike tours of the dunes, but for something different, arrive after dark and spend time staring up at the night sky. You'll have a* traditional Cape Verdean dinner in your camp before heading out with a guide to gaze up at the Milky Way and beyond. The naked eye is enough to observe the constellations, thanks to no light pollution, but telescopes are also provided and activities put on for kids." (Canning, A. 2022)

"Deserto de Viana with Sign" by Felitsata is licensed under CC BY-SA 3.0.

Egypt

Crime Rate: 46.57

Cost of Living Index: 29.52

Quality of Life Index: 89.87

Health Care Index: 47.01

Visa requirement for US citizens: Visa on arrival for 1 month

Visa requirement for UK citizens: Visa on arrival for 1 month

Visa requirement for Israel citizens: Visa required

If you read my first book, you will have read that my belief was that ancient Sandboarding originated here; it doesn't help that nowadays the country is much bigger than its Nile centred civilization days. The territory it acquired is mostly a barren far eastern part of the Sahara which lies in the west of the country, the Great Sand Sea can only be described as a sizeable rural expanse of the Sahara that spreads across both Egypt & Libya that contains consistently high altitude sand dunes that combined with the solitude of a few nomadic residents, make this the ideal place for recreational sport in a peaceful environment, I included Egypt instead of Libya because of the current political situation and that it's hugely taxing if not impossible to get in Libya as a tourist; you'll also find that Egypt is visited by a lot of tourists every year for oddly enough, Sandboarding; as it turns out, a lot of adventure seekers visit Sandboarding's true home after all. However, Egypt is almost entirely desert so you could, theoretically Sandboard anywhere.

"EgSandSeaDune" by Roland Unger is licensed under CC BY-SA 3.0.

Kenya

Crime Rate: 56.21

Cost of Living Index: 33.92

Quality of Life Index: 92.54

Health Care Index: 63.4

Visa requirement for US citizens: E-visa valid for 3 months

Visa requirement for UK citizens: E-visa valid for 3 months

Visa requirement for Israel citizens: E-visa valid for 3 months

I didn't believe that Kenya had sand dunes either but at the same time I was pleased only because it broke away from deserts and beaches; thankfully the Loibor Seder dune is in neither. If it's any benefit, the dune lies close to Mount Ng'iro not far south of Lake Turkana; this dune in Marsabit county is the highest in Kenya and is a well known hiking area among locals and the lucky few foreigners who get to come here. Near the dune, there isn't a tourist camp but given its isolation, I'd highly hope you'd prepare for the trip. "*The dune is a pleasant attraction, that would take the average person 8 to 15 minutes to get to the top. 10 to 15 minutes taking photos and resting. Another, 5 minutes coming down. This would provide a 30 minutes excursion as a part of a longer itinerary. Our guests, enroute to Tuum, Mt Kulal and Kargi never miss the attraction. The Loibor Seder dune complex occurs between two hills, the sand collects on the southern hill. The hills are part of the continuation of the Matthew ranges, that become Ndoto mountains and later, Nyiro mountains."* (Begin North Adventures, n.d.) I apologise for the lack of decent imagery on the dunes, but I did source a distant image of the area from Lake Turkana.

"Lake Turkana 01" by Jeffmugendi is licensed under CC BY-SA 4.0.

Madagascar

Crime Rate: Not Known

Cost of Living Index: Not Known

Quality of Life Index: Not Known

Health Care Index: Not Known

Visa requirement for US citizens: Visa on arrival for 3 months

Visa requirement for UK citizens: Visa on arrival for 3 months

Visa requirement for Israel citizens: Visa on arrival for 3 months

Another one of those countries where I was pleasantly surprised to see an appearance when it comes to Sandboarding, but yet again for the world's 4th largest island in area I should have expected some sand dunes on Madagascar. In this book, I have sourced 2 places that are ideal for Sandboarding on Madagascar and both of them are on the South of the island, the first is a small town called Faux Cap also known as Betanty; which is on the southernmost tip of the island, the trouble is with a lot of the country, due to climate change and the lack of suitable rainfall and irrigation, there is not enough water and the shifting sands make agriculture more difficult; "*But sand and wind movements are not the only symptoms of extreme weather worsened by climate change in this part of the world. The sea itself is changing, and fishing conditions have deteriorated. People like Ranobolee, whose livelihoods were once reliant on fishing, have had to switch to agriculture. However, cassava and maize fields are no longer as productive and reliable as before due to a lack of rainfall.*" (Rahmoun, A. 2021) The image below is of the area; however it was taken in the 1970s, looking elsewhere the nearby beach had a significant presence of higher dunes, and this image was the only royalty free one I could find.

"Madagascar74.135" by Madagascar74 is licensed under CC BY-SA 3.0.

Still in the South of the country, another sandboarding destination that's significantly less touristy but is the subject of scientific mystery; there are rows of "chevrons" in the far South of Madagascar. *"For nearly a decade, geologist Dallas Abbott and her colleagues have been trying to prove that an enormous space rock, possibly an asteroid, smashed into the Indian Ocean about 10,000 years ago and created a megatsunami, a set of giant waves that washed over the east coast of Africa. Such a tsunami could have created waves as high as 300 feet (91 meters)—three times larger than the Indian Ocean tsunami in 2004 that left 230,000 dead."* (Casey, M. 2015)

The theory is that these chevrons are the result of Mega-tsunami's that were the results of space matter that hit the Indian Ocean and the chevrons that were formed, are shifting lands shaped by the waves. The Ampalaza Chevron, a 3 and a half hour drive from Ampanihy, a town on the nearest highway. The Chevron looks like the sand was pushed inland for a few kilometres. Not a lot of infrastructure exists in this area of the country and tourism isn't massive, a lot of geologists and geographers are the area's primary visitors and adventure travelers are most undoubtedly unheard of.

"ISS027-E-17959 - View of Madagascar" by Earth Science and Remote Sensing Unit is a public domain work.

Mauritania

Crime Rate: Not Known

Cost of Living Index: Not Known

Quality of Life Index: Not Known

Health Care Index: Not Known

Visa requirement for US citizens: Visa on arrival

Visa requirement for UK citizens: Visa on arrival

Visa requirement for Israel citizens: Visa on arrival

A known fact is that over three-quarters of Mauritania is desert, and when it comes to farming less than 1% of land is arable. The majority of the country is covered in sand; therefore, there isn't a shortage of dunes ready for adventure tourists; the town of Chinguetti has been designated by the Mauritanian government as a tourist hot spot. The U.S. Peace Corps is also stationed in the area; hoping to preserve peace for these tourists so tourists can participate in surfing down the dunes, and visiting the city's libraries, after all this city is also known as the "City of Libraries". "*As pilgrims and scholars came and went, many left religious texts, scientific studies and historical manuscripts. In fact, so many of these historical documents accumulated over the years that during Chinguetti's peak between the 13th and 17th Centuries, this thriving city boasted 30 libraries."* (Khrustaleva, O. 2020) Chinguetti's tourism industry has been threatened by terrorism previously, but with terrorism becoming a gradual thing of the past in this country, the threat appears to have subsided. The nation's hoping that the few tourists that Mauritania receives, they will pay this city, which also happens to be a UNESCO World Heritage Site, a much needed visit.

"Chinguetti dunes" by Radosław Botev is licensed under CC BY 3.0.

Morocco

Crime Rate: 49.07

Cost of Living Index: 33.83

Quality of Life Index: 107.54

Health Care Index: 46.69 (lowest in Africa)

Visa requirement for US citizens: No visa required for 3 months

Visa requirement for UK citizens: No visa required for 3 months

Visa requirement for Israel citizens: Visa required

Morocco is a country on the North African coast that receives a lot of tourists each year and it has come a long way since its independence, with the majority coming from France and Spain. The city of Agadir is the largest seaside resort in Morocco and the majority of the city's inhabitants speak Berber as their first language. An hour's drive to the north from Agadir, you can find the Taboga dunes; and around the same distance to the South from Agadir, you will end up in the Souss-Massa National Park, both of these sites will have plenty of dunes for recreation however in the Souss-Massa National Park, you'll find plenty of wildlife and some lakes so activity will be a lot more restrictive in parts of the protected park area.

"Marokko- Agadir- Dünen im Süden der Bucht - panoramio" by Gottfried Hoffmann is licensed under CC BY 3.0.

Mozambique

Crime Rate: 62.8

Cost of Living Index: Not Known

Quality of Life Index: Not Known

Health Care Index: Not Known

Visa requirement for US citizens: Visa on arrival for 1 month

Visa requirement for UK citizens: Visa on arrival for 1 month

Visa requirement for Israel citizens: Visa on arrival for 1 month

I am still pleasantly surprised by Mozambique's appearance in the first book, so I must remind everyone that Mozambique is home to the dunes of Bazaruto Island and one of the few Portuguese-speaking countries on the continent. The island that sits just to the South of Bazaruto is Benguerra Island, and the resort of Kisawa on the island has been highlighted as a must-see tourist spot not just for Mozambique but for the whole of Africa. Diving and exploring the dunes are top activities on either of these islands: "*Any guest embarking on the journey to get here, the resort recognizes, must have a desire for exploration. So Kisawa indulges it: Activities include overnight glamping on the dunes, sunset cocktails on a traditional dhow, and expeditions to spot dugongs (rare sea cows). Kisawa partners with the Bazaruto Center for Scientific Studies (BCSS), the continent's first-ever permanent ocean observatory, also founded by Flohr, so you can join scientists on coral-monitoring dives or help them tag sharks from research vessels."* (Taylor, E. 2022)

"Bazaruto - I (23918326530)" by Cornelius Kibelka is licensed under CC BY-SA 2.0.

Namibia

Crime Rate: 64.7

Cost of Living Index: Not Known

Quality of Life Index: Not Known

Health Care Index: Not Known

Visa requirement for US citizens: No visa required for 3 months

Visa requirement for UK citizens: No visa required for 3 months

Visa requirement for Israel citizens: Visa required

As I write this I have yet to go to Namibia; however, once you read this I most likely will have visited as I have booked tickets and will have a Namibian sandboarding adventure with friends in March 2023, just in time for my birthday. The main reasons for visiting don't include the historic and European-influenced cities of Windhoek & Swakopmund, but rather the many sand dunes in the Namib Desert. The first dune I shall document here is "Dune 7", the highest dune in Namibia as described by the Namibian Ministry of Environment & Tourism. "*The 1,256-foot dune got its name because it is the seventh dune past the Tsauchab River, which runs through part of the Namib Desert. The desert itself, believed to be dry for at least 55 million years, is considered the oldest in the world."* (Fox News, 2018)

"Dune 7" by MrsKuhn7373 is licensed under CC BY-SA 4.0.

Located approximately a five-hour drive from Dune 7 and travelling south from Swakopmund, you can find another significant reason to see Namibia. The vast expanses of land known as a "Vlei", these are shallow lakes which can sometimes degrade over time to a salt or clay pan, Sossusvlei in Namibia is an excellent example of a vlei that is both a salt and clay pan; the area of Sossusvlei is home to dunes around the vlei known as

"Dune 45" because it lies 45 kilometres past Sesriem on the road to Sossusvlei and another called "Big Daddy" that's the highest in the area. If you're planning on hitting the dunes in the Namib-Naukluft National Park area, the best advice is: "*If you want to climb the dunes, Big Mama Dune, Big Daddy Dune and Dune 45 are some of the tallest. Note: The slippery, hot sand is tough to manage. Visiting early in the morning means the sand is less scalding and will be easier to climb.*" (Zaino, L. 2022)

"Sossusvlei" by Ikiwaner is a GNU General Public License work.

Nigeria

Crime Rate: 63.84

Cost of Living Index: 30.49

Quality of Life Index: 52.44 (lowest in this book)

Health Care Index: 48.49

Visa requirement for US citizens: Visa required

Visa requirement for UK citizens: Visa required

Visa requirement for Israel citizens: Visa required

Another surprise found in this book, Nigeria is the largest economy in Africa and indeed a country that is home to sand dunes. Given its location, Nigeria has many ports and flat coasts, but the sand dunes that lie in Nigeria are more closer to its northern border with Niger. Yobe State has a nickname of "Pride of the Sahel" and it's easy to see why Tulotulo and Yusufari are examples of the best dunes in this state. Back in the 2010s, the terrorist group Boko Haram was active in this area of Nigeria. But since then, the group has decreased dramatically and their operations are practically over; tourism to Yobe State is fuelled in no small part thanks to the sand dunes in this state, the experience by a writer from New Telegraph sums it up nicely: "*The safari drive started at 10.40am from the palace and it took over an hour before we got in contact with the dunes. Beautiful sight to behold as we inched our way through the expanse of dunes. At that moment they were the most beautiful thing that we had ever set our eyes on. The guide has different locations for different types and features of the sand dunes. While the first location we approached had a brownish colour, we got to other part where what we saw could be described as mysterious. There were about four colours of dunes that didn't mix with one another. It was magical, delightsome and exciting to behold.*" (Yotamara, U.C. 2022)

"Tulutulu in yobe state Nigeria" by Atbalah is licensed under CC BY-SA 4.0.

Senegal

Crime Rate: Not Known

Cost of Living Index: 50.25 (highest in Africa)

Quality of Life Index: Not Known

Health Care Index: Not Known

Visa requirement for US citizens: No visa required for 3 months

Visa requirement for UK citizens: No visa required for 3 months

Visa requirement for Israel citizens: Visa on arrival for 3 months

Senegal borders Mauritania which we've already seen is plagued with desert; however Senegal also has an area of desert in the north of the country, however it lies south of the Senegal River which if you look at a map, you'll find that Africa tends to get greener closer to the equator. The Lompoul Desert is named after the nearby settlement of Lompoul and lies roughly halfway between the Mauritanian border and Dakar, Senegal's capital. I found out about this desert thanks to a 2010 film called "End Of The Road" where Alexis Dubus and Sy Thomas drive from England to the Gambia and cross through deserts along the way, I highly suggest you watch it. The Lompoul Desert is popular among Senegalese tourists and given the landscape here compared to the rest of Senegal, content creator and travel blogger Dev Walker was amazed with how much Senegal had to offer in an interview with Forbes: "*From the beaches in Saly, to the busy city of Dakar, the desert in Lompoul, and the mangroves in Fatick ... I was blown away by how so many areas were so different that you would've thought you were in multiple countries instead of one.*" (Good, R. 2022)

"Lompoul1 by G.No is licensed under CC BY 2.0.

South Africa

Crime Rate: 76.06 (highest in Africa)

Cost of Living Index: 42.09

Quality of Life Index: 136.02 (highest in Africa)

Health Care Index: 63.97

Visa requirement for US citizens: No visa required for 3 months

Visa requirement for UK citizens: No visa required for 3 months

Visa requirement for Israel citizens: No visa required for 3 months

If you recall earlier in the book, you were given six unique places in the USA; you're also going to have six spectacular spots in South Africa, but the country with the most individual sites has yet to be seen in this book so stick around... South Africa despite its troubled past with its apartheid policy and high rates of crime continues to give a bad image to some foreign tourists visiting. However, South Africa has excellent sites for Sandboarding and adventure sportspeople across its lengthy coastline. Hence, there's truly something for everyone here, whether your activity is on land, in the air, or at sea. Starting in the largest city of Johannesburg which lies in the landlocked province of Gauteng you'd be forgiven for thinking there's no sand dunes there. Still, you'd be mistaken when you lay your eyes on "Mount Mayhem" which is only a 20 minute drive from O.R. Tambo International Airport. Sadly, I have no free images of these dunes as they're small but to give context as to where they are, I've included a photo of Johannesburg and when you look at this image; just think, how on earth would I be able to sandboard here?

"Joburg top by Zakysant is licensed under CC BY-SA 3.0.

Leaving the city and venturing a little to west to the Northern Cape, Witsand which isn't to be confused with a small coastal town of the same name, is a national park that covers 3,500 hectares of land which is home to many sand dunes including those with singing sands. The sands here are the perfect height to hit the dunes as they don't feel too high to climb yet aren't too high that you get short of breath. If the dunes tire you out, the other well known activity is watching the many wild animals on a game reserve, bird-watching, and stargazing. Camping is also big business around here so for the truly authentic safari and sporting experience, I'd suggest a few days camping in their reinforced canvas tents, which are a world of luxury compared to a standard tent. It's also a good idea to spend a few days on the dunes and watching the animals all the while watching the stars at night. The entire park at Witsand is dominated by dunes over 1,200 above sea level.

"Witsand, Northern Cape, South Africa (20351950068) by South African Tourism is licensed under CC BY 2.0.

Away from Johannesburg and the North, and to South Africa's other big city of Cape Town, just 45 kilometres away is the gorgeous dunes at Atlantis, next to the Koeberg Nature Reserve. I mentioned these dunes in the previous book. I did include that these dunes are often used in the cinematic industry, used in several movies but what I should have included in my last book was that you can see Table Mountain. This famous mountain overlooks Cape Town itself. The best activities aside from Sandboarding are quad-biking, and paragliding; much like other dunes in this book, a lot of emphasis is put on photo-shoots if you decide not to do any sport. Despite being outside the big city, many keen athletes come here for its sporting value and may even be considered a sandboarding jewel of Africa.

"Ladybirdsandboarding by Bongani2 is licensed under CC BY-SA 3.0.

Mossel Bay which is in the east of the Western Cape province, it's not a busy tourist town. Still, residents do live in the area all year round, not just in December & January (in the southern hemisphere, the summer months are flipped) a lot of the visitors will arrive here for walking tours to see the town's history, to see architecture unique to the rest of South Africa and prehistoric archaeology from native people from the area; the few visitors who visit the dunes will be given a unique experience of 3 dunes of the Mossel Bay Dragon Dunes system, this could be a contender for the best sandboarding site in not just Africa but possibly the world… I'll let you, the readers decide that. You are given the three dunes that are the "Baby", "Big Boy", and "Dragon" dunes that gradually increase in excitement and adrenaline; from their own website. "*Dragon Dune is 170 metres high and provides rides of up to 350 metres long, which overwhelms all competition in South Africa! Maximum speeds of 90km/h have been reached on a belly board!*" (Dragon Dune Sandboarding, n.d.) I cannot find a better snapshot but I have found smaller dunes on Mossel Bay, so you'll see the actual dunes and you shall be in awe when the dunes are staring back at you.

"Diaz Beach, Mossel Bay by rcbutcher is a public domain work.

One province across, before we do a round trip and eventually arrive back at Jozi where we started our South African voyage. Nahoon Beach is a short drive from another big city in South Africa, East London; it is the most popular beach in the East London area. It's the best place if you're a swimmer or a surfer; it's South Africa's answer to England's Fistral Beach or Australia's Bondi Beach. Nahoon Beach and its dunes aren't too flat and the cliffs are close to the seaside, the dunes are incredibly steep when you look at its angles, and the rocky cliffs aren't too far away from some of the further out dunes, but so far it's absolutely the smallest of the sand dunes in this list for South Africa.

"2005-03-08 10-24-17 South Africa - Blue Bend" by Hansueli Krapf is licensed under CC BY-SA 3.0.

Finally going up to KwaZulu-Natal where we find a town just over 200km from the nation's border with Eswatini (Swaziland) is a village of just over a thousand residents where hippos roam the streets at night, due to the nearby iSimangaliso Wetland Park. The nearby dunes are given the prestigious title "The Highest Vegetated Sand Dunes in Africa" which of course to the advanced sportsperson, height matters. On it's main beach there exist small dunes for those just starting out but venturing into the abyss is only recommended for those who are eager enough for the sights and to see the park in its entirety. "*Fringing the 280km coastline of this natural World Heritage Site are sand dunes exceeding 180m in height. These impressive dunes have been built and sculptured by the wind over the past 25 000 to 30 000 years. Rising steeply from the waves of the Indian Ocean are the highest vegetated dunes in Africa. The dunes are composed of windblown sand driven off the beach by north-easterly winds. Vegetation growing on the dunes form a delicate membrane of plant life. These plants trap nutrients and stabilise the dunes. On the seaward side, the dunes have a stunted forest whereas on the leeward side a large Climax forest can be found. Hardwood trees in the climax can exceed 20m. Growing on these trees are a variety of epiphytic plants, including orchids, ferns, cactus (natural to Africa) and lichen (old man's beard). A network of lianas and creepers complete this remarkable habitat. Within this unique habitat occurs a variety of birds, monkeys, reptiles, squirrels, antelope and insects. Visitors can access this area by utilising guided safaris or self-guided walks.*" (St Lucia, n.d.) And for such a detailed description, that's put South Africa on a high note!

"St Lucia Main Beach 01" by Ossewa is licensed under CC BY-SA 4.0.

Tunisia

Crime Rate: 44.29 (lowest in Africa)

Cost of Living Index: 27.87

Quality of Life Index: 114.56

Health Care Index: 56.54

Visa requirement for US citizens: No visa required for 3 months

Visa requirement for UK citizens: No visa required for 3 months

Visa requirement for Israel citizens: Visa required

An obscure reason this country will always be known to me is that Tunisia's independence day and my birthday happened to fall on the same day (20 March). The film fans reading this may also know that the scenes of Luke Skywalker's home planet of Tatooine was filmed in this country; even more intriguing is that this first destination is in the Tataouine Governate which is in the far South of the country. The outpost of Ksar Ghilane isn't just an oasis and archaeological site but a historic site that played a vital role in the Battle of Tunisia during the Second World War, Ksar Ghilane is also the gateway to the Sahara as it serves as the easternmost point of the Grand

Erg Oriental, a vast sand sea covering Algeria and Tunisia; If you have concerns regarding the safety of the country following the revolution and terrorist attacks in the 2010s; fear not; compared to other countries in this book, Tunisia has the lowest known crime rate among African nations in this book. "*Ksar Ghilane is now also a base for desert tourism. Among other activities, it is possible to travel by camel to the nearby Roman fort of Tisavar, built during the reign of Commodus in late 2nd century. This ancient fort is why this oasis camp is still referred to as a ksar. But today there is no need for military fortifications here. Unlike almost all other north African countries, Tunisia's desert is free from armed groups.*" (Johnstone, H. 2018)

"Ksar Ghilane (4103846788)" by veroyama is licensed under CC BY 2.0.

If you go west on the map, you'll find a significant water source in the middle of Tunisia; it isn't water but a salt lake, the Chott El Djerid. Part of Chott El Djerid lies in the Tozeur Province, the least populated in all of Tunisia; Tataouine is second least populated. The city of Tozeur and the outskirts make the perfect destination for those wanting a genuine and traditional Berber experience, the dunes which engulf the city and due to the success of agriculture, many people live here. The place feels more metropolitan compared to further South where the setting is more nomadic. "*Nestled amid luscious palm-tree-dotted mountains, breathtaking waterfalls, giant sand dunes and wide canyons, this desert city is filled with an array of date, citrus, peach and fig trees, the fruits of which are plucked and eaten or turned into essential oils and perfumes for tourists to take home."* (Gervais, E. 2022) The city is flooded with organisations that will happily provide a Sandboarding and off-road experience without too much expense.

"Tozeur traces" by Margarita Modroño is licensed under CC BY-SA 4.0.

Oceania

We come to the last continent on our trip; I feel bad for this part of the world because it's far out to reach for a lot of people and because I've only managed to put in 4 countries from this part of the world, the majority of the sand dunes are in Australia. Some dunes I've included in my 100 come from outside Australia, so I feel relieved that I can show something other than just Australia here. People are getting financially better off; therefore, going to this part of the globe is getting more affordable and realistic for many people. Despite being the smallest continent in size and population, the quality offered cannot possibly compare to anywhere else on the planet.

Australia

Crime Rate: 43.85

Cost of Living Index: 77.75 (highest in Oceania)

Quality of Life Index: 183.81 (highest in Oceania)

Health Care Index: 78.14 (highest in Oceania)

Visa requirement for US citizens: E-visa valid for 3 months

Visa requirement for UK citizens: E-visa valid for 3 months

Visa requirement for Israel citizens: E-visa required

The United States has 6 sandboarding sites in this book, as does South Africa; however, there are seven for Australia! So this will undoubtedly be the largest segment. Still, for a country that's also the 6th largest in the world by land area that's mostly covered by desert, it all becomes clear that Australia has a lot to offer the average sandboarding aficionado. The very first stop will be in Western Australia. The dunes of Lancelin, on the roadside of the appropriately named "Indian Ocean Drive", are the dunes that lie and have been a critical location for those on quad bikes, driving off-roaders, the ever-growing kitesurfing community, and even the tiny but humble sandboarding community. The sandboarding following may be small globally; however, in this part of Australia, you'll likely find someone to rent or sell one to you during the peak season. "*This 200km drive may sound intense, but the gorgeous natural landscapes and enchanting wildlife will make it all worth it. Start your first full day by driving to the Lancelin Sand Dunes, where you can sandboard down the dunes; the drive up from Perth is fairly short at 1.5 - 2hrs. Stop by the Lancelin General Store on your way to the dunes to rent a sandboard. Sandboard rentals cost just AUD 12.50 for 2.5 hours, so you can spend the morning without worrying about breaking the bank. Reserve your boards beforehand, especially if you're visiting during the peak season.*" (Bumidin, Q. 2022)

"Dunes at Lancelin" by RustyHistory is licensed under CC BY-SA 4.0.

Leaving Western Australia and heading to South Australia's mainland, we end up near questionable towns such as Smoky Bay and Streaky Bay. The destination in question we're looking at here is Yanerbie; the sand dunes here are a haven for children looking to get their energy out as they explore the highs and lows of the area's dunes. The Dunes of Yanerbie are situated on the western coast of the Eyre Peninsula, and in this area, farming and fishing are the most prominent industries. Hence, it makes the perfect opportunity to have a day on the dunes and consume a lot of local produce when it turns to the evening. Unfortunately, I couldn't find the dunes up close, but you can see them from space, and if you can see the dunes above the earth, you know they're big.

"ISS006-E-18786 - View of South Australia" by Earth Science and Remote Sensing Unit is a public domain work.

Off the mainland, and if you've read my first book, it'll be familiar; Kangaroo Island sits off the coast of South Australia; the dunes can be up to 70 metres above the sea, which, for an island, the sea will be all around. Many people don't come to the island for the adventures and the thrills of sandboarding but rather to see the nature that lies on the island, which includes bees, koalas, seals, and, shockingly, kangaroos! The dunes are challenging enough here that Australian Winter Olympic athletes train on these dunes, and if Australia can win a gold medal at the 2022 games in Beijing, then they're good enough for a part-time sandboarder from England. As you may be aware, the pandemic was a nail in the coffin for many small businesses, but not for Little Sahara, which operates Sandboarding and Dune Tours owned by local Brenton Davis. Brenton's company was lucky to thrive despite a pandemic just after wildfires hit the island. "*Fortunately for Brenton and Little Sahara, South Australians were not banned from travelling within their own state — and when they did visit during the pandemic, it wasn't just for the day or a long weekend.* "*With hardly any intrastate restrictions, South Aussies would visit for a week or two at a time during the pandemic, which was wonderful,*" *said Davis.* "*It gave them the chance to explore the island properly at a more leisurely pace, rather than trying to cram everything the island has to offer in a day or two.*'" (Smithson, B. 2022)

"Little Sahara - panoramio (5)" by photophat is licensed under CC BY 3.0.

Before I go back to the mainland and if you venture on the water and dock on Tasmania, you conveniently arrive at another great sandboarding spot; the Henty dunes are on the west coast, entirely opposite the metropolis of Hobart, Tasmania's capital. The Henty dune system isn't tall when you look at the other dunes in Australia; however, the area covered by the dunes here is larger than the Dune of Pilat in France. A picnic area is situated near the side, away from the sea but lacks toilet and water facilities; surfing in Tasmania and the rest of Australia is something that naturally happens; there are many beaches in Australia to explore, and when it comes to Henty, it's not just the sea that offers an adrenaline rush: "*When the water's choppy, try sandboarding on dunes across the country, often in places with rich Aboriginal history, like Henty Dunes in Tasmania.*" (Tang, P. 2022)

"Henty Dunes - 2013.04 - panoramio" by rheins is licensed under CC BY 3.0.

Journeying from Tasmania, skipping Victoria and heading straight into New South Wales, a great surfing spot is Stockton Beach. Stockton Beach is the most historically significant site in all of Oceania on this list; the beach was fortified in case of a Japanese attack during the Second World War. A small but strong-willed residential community that lives on the coast in small shacks prohibited from being rebuilt, known as "Tin City", a portion of the area has banned driving due to its cultural and historical significance with the aborigine community. The beach has been a sanctuary for many sports events for all land, air, and sea. It is also necessary that a permit is obtained to use vehicles on some parts of the dunes; Stockton Beach is part of the Hunter Valley, as the river of the same name is close by and not too far from Port Stephens and Newcastle. *"Created thousands of years ago, the dunes are 30 metres high—as tall as 10-storeyed buildings—stretching over 30 km of spectacular coastline, from Birubi Beach to Newcastle. "The dunes are constantly changing; the next time you visit, it will be a completely different landscape," says our local guide. From the top of the towering dunes, one can see far up to Newcastle, and maybe spot wild kangaroos on a lucky day."* (Sunder, K. 2022) Before I show the photo, it's worth mentioning that surfing is possible, but it's not recommended because tank traps in the water and surfing with tank traps in the ocean are perilous.

"Stockton Beach (8333174474)" by Phil Whitehouse is licensed under CC BY 2.0.

Going upstate in Queensland and on a beautifully named town Rainbow Beach, the dunes that sit here just south of Fraser Island, which the island also has dunes. 3 hours north of Brisbane, Queensland's capital; the dunes I want to include for this part aren't strictly dunes but more a sand blow, which is what gives some dunes a bowl or a crescent shape due to many factors, be it wind, underground water, an earthquake, substandard geology, etc... The British reading this may be aware that this can be seen at Holywell Bay when you visit some dunes there; the dunes here are a part of the town's identity as tourism is an essential factor in the local economy; this is also partly because these dunes sit in the Cooloola Recreational Area, and also making these dunes like some others in this book, these dunes used to be a forest: "*The 15ha sandblow, part of the huge accumulation of windblown sand known as the Cooloola sandmass, is slowly creeping westward, burying everything in its wake with sand. Where we once stood over 10 years ago in the forest has now been completely engulfed.*" (Sinclair, S. 2022)

"Footprints Carlo Sand Blow (33160372018)" by Theo Crazzolara is licensed under CC BY 2.0.

And finally, in this massive country in both book space and dune variety, we meet a dune with a specific name: Big Red in the Simpson Desert. The local area and the dune stand tall, not too far from the state border with South Australia, and for context, the nearest town of Birdsville is in Queensland. The dune has had an unusual recent history as it played home to a music festival despite being many miles away from the nearest big city. Recently, a couple decided to tie the knot atop a dune 40 metres above the ground. "*Karen and Anthony Maximui from Gippsland ditched the traditional wedding and instead climbed the Simpson Desert's highest sand dune to exchange vows in front of a sprawling crowd. The loved-up pair said getting married at the isolated festival, 38 kilometres from Birdsville, was always part of the plan but there was an element of adventure to it.*" (Pengilley, V. 2022) Aside from music festivals and a wedding, motocross is commonplace on these dunes due to the desert setting, and you'll most likely come across motorbikes rather than a sandboarder. Temperatures aren't shy to go above the 40 degrees Centigrade mark (104 Fahrenheit), so you'll need plenty of water and a massive hat as an absolute minimum.

"BigRed" by Phanly is licensed under CC BY 3.0.

Fiji

Crime Rate: 55.63 (highest in Oceania)

Cost of Living Index: 43.16 (lowest in Oceania)

Quality of Life Index: Not Known

Health Care Index: Not Known

Visa requirement for US citizens: No visa required for 4 months

Visa requirement for UK citizens: No visa required for 4 months

Visa requirement for Israel citizens: No visa required for 4 months

A very well-known tourist island nation for those in Australia & New Zealand due to the close distance between the countries. Fiji is one of the more developed countries in the Pacific region that doesn't have to rely on as much foreign aid from the Commonwealth of Nations & China. The Sigatoka Sand Dunes are a must-see sight on the country's largest island Viti Levu. The Sigatoka Dunes are a hit with not just foreign visitors but also the Flying Fijians (the name of the national rugby team), as the Fijian rugby sevens team won 2 back to back titles thanks in part to these dunes during the 2016 and 2020 Olympic Games. The dunes are under 70 kilometres away from Nadi International Airport and 130 kilometres away from Suva, Fiji's capital; "*The big island is also home to the awe-inspiring Sigatoka Sand Dunes, which are located one of the country's few national parks. These impressive national formations range from 20 to 60 meters tall and formed over thousands of years; the park is also a designated UNESCO world heritage site.*" (Shepert, E. 2022) The island has much to see in terms of nature, lush green forests and rolling hills that overlook a coral reef coast, and the sandy dunes that pour into the Pacific are just an added bonus to the nation's natural beauty.

"SigatokaDunesFiji" by RodBland is licensed under CC BY 2.0.

New Zealand

Crime Rate: 43.3 (lowest in Oceania)

Cost of Living Index: 74.52

Quality of Life Index: 176.81 (lowest in Oceania)

Health Care Index: 73.32 (lowest in Oceania)

Visa requirement for US citizens: E-visa valid for 3 months

Visa requirement for UK citizens: E-visa valid for 6 months

Visa requirement for Israel citizens: E-visa valid for 3 months

"*From pristine beaches and lush native forests to rugged mountains and clear blue lakes, New Zealand's outdoors really can't be beaten. After analysing the number of natural features like volcanoes, coral reefs, tropical rainforests and glaciers per 100,000 square kilometres, money.co.uk crowned Indonesia as 'the world's most naturally beautiful country'.*" (Pollok, S. 2022) That came from a 2022 survey that crowned Indonesia as the world's most naturally beautiful country; New Zealand came second. Considering its' size, it should have won; this may also be why it has topped the Sandboarding Nation Top 10 Countries for Sandboarding list back to back. There is a reasonable degree of decent places to get your rush on while you're here but by far the most talked about and most well known even by people outside of New Zealand is the dune area of Te Paki, near Cape Reinga in the far north of the North Island. For many sandboarding die-hards, Te Paki is a place that has to be seen to be believed; "*It's even harder to believe your eyes once you get there. Te Paki Giant Sand Dunes is far from being a single, pitiful hill of sand. It's a whole 10km long and 1km wide strip of dunes rising up to 150m. A real desert with no beginning and no end. The sand here is very unusual. Despite the wind, somehow, it's not all in your eyes, mouth and hair. It politely stays where your feet are, allowing you to admire the views with no side effect of choking to death.*" (Spodyneiko, K. 2020)

"Te Paki Sand Dunes, New Zealand (9)" by Michal Klajban is licensed under CC BY-SA 4.0.

Vanuatu

Crime Rate: Not Known

Cost of Living Index: Not Known

Quality of Life Index: Not Known

Health Care Index: Not Known

Visa requirement for US citizens: No visa required for 1 month

Visa requirement for UK citizens: No visa required for 1 month

Visa requirement for Israel citizens: No visa required for 1 month

And now, the 100th destination of no particular order of preference in this book; is on another pacific island nation; this one isn't a dune but another volcano that can be perfectly acceptable for the sandboarding guru or anyone willing to give it their best shot. In my last book, I said that Mount Yasur on Tanna Island has erupted continuously since 1774, and one completed book later, it's still erupting. I have found some interesting stories that you don't volcano board your way down. Still, according to one news source, ash board: *Accessible by a short, easy climb to the top, travellers can find themselves at the top of Mt. Yasur's impressive crater for a once-in-*

a-lifetime, front-row natural firework display. If that's not enough of an adrenaline boost, you can also ashboard down the side of the volcano after you reach the summit." (Karryon, 2022) I'm not sure why ash was chosen; maybe 'volcano' sounded too scary. Also, what's impressive is that I have yet to see any location in this book with this next feature. Mount Yasur is the only volcano with a functional postbox at the top, so you could have an instant camera and a postage stamp and send a postcard on a scale of 'cool' the world has never seen. Tanna Island, where Yasur is located, is a 40-minute plane ride from the nation's capital, Port-Vila.

"Yasur2" by Benutzer:Plenz is licensed under CC BY-SA 3.0.

And that concludes my Top 100 of the World's Greatest Sandboarding Destinations.

Honourable Mentions

This is the part of the book where I include some of the decent enough dunes in my belief that it would have been included in my Top 100 list should something have gone wrong. I, of course, can't include everywhere on the planet, so I'm likely to get moaned at by somebody but give me a break; I've already listed 100 places from 65 countries. All would be worthy of inclusion, but I limited myself to a hundred.

Angola's city of Moçâmedes is one of the small pockets of the Namib Desert that spill over into Angola; the city is a fair distance from the border with Namibia, which is one of the major port cities of Angola. The dunes completely surround the city, and to the South of the city, the Iona National Park, the largest National park in Angola, will be found here, along with many rare types of trees and differing kinds of vegetation that blend in well with the dunes and the Mars-like desert landscape.

Kenya has more than one sand dune area; the biggest in the country made my list but the dunes of Lamu Island and the village of Shella, which sits atop the dunes on the island. Dunes on the coast make up the bulk of the island of Lamu, and with sandy grass-covered hills in the middle of the island, they compose an area of just under 10 square kilometres. When we talk about the people of Lamu Island, many communities of Arabs, Europeans, Asians, and Africans have, at some point, called the island home; and each has left its unique mark.

Finally, the Kvitsanden is the only known sandy dune and preserved Norwegian area with such geological features. It is the only shifting sand area in all of Norway, and honestly, it's not tall; there's no point comparing it to Dune 7 or Federico Kirbus, as it's just over 10 metres high. There wouldn't be many purposes for including the Kvitsanden dune in my list because not just the height, not just because it's inland, but primarily because of the temperature due to how north Norway is on the earth.

Final Thoughts

Since the last book was published, there have been a lot of questions I wanted to ask myself when it came to writing this; many of these questions resulted from things I realised when I published The Sandboarding Book. I decided to make a second book because I wanted to elaborate on where Sandboarding takes place; there was once a mention on Wikipedia that the sport takes place in over 30 countries; my mission was to disprove that and provide some evidence that there were more. There are 190+ sovereign states in the world, and admittedly, countries such as the Vatican would have more helipads and TV stations per head than anywhere else but no sand dunes. Nations that I wouldn't usually think of, such as Albania & Botswana, wouldn't have been included unless extensive research had been conducted.

This book was written to serve as a travel guide and additional information on where Sandboarding can be practised worldwide. I'm relatively good at world geography, and I've travelled in my time despite only visiting three of the sites in this book. Sandboarding travel isn't something I would otherwise do due to the expense of transporting a Sandboard on a plane. I wanted to show that even far-out nations and countries that wouldn't typically be considered dune hosting are just as worthy of being good places for Sandboarding. Despite rates of crime and costs of living that may look more attractive elsewhere, if your gut tells you that you want to see somewhere and the opportunity comes, my advice would be to take it. I don't have one favourite destination from the book. However, Europe would most definitely be for beginners and those looking to be well-connected to amenities and people. I would love to visit Namibia, South Africa, and Australia for Sandboarding. The top countries I'd like to see in general are Japan, Vietnam, Brazil, and Egypt; the sandboarding potential is primarily an unexpected bonus I'd, of course, partake of if I were there.

References

Visalist (n.d.) Where can you travel with USA passport in 2022. Retrieved from Visalist: https://visalist.io/united-states-of-america/ (Accessed: 29th June 2022)

Visalist (n.d.) Where can you travel with UK passport in 2022. Retrieved from Visalist: https://visalist.io/united-kingdom/ (Accessed: 29th June 2022)

Visalist (n.d.) Where can you travel with Israel passport in 2022. Retrieved from Visalist: https://visalist.io/israel/ (Accessed: 29th June 2022)

Numbeo (n.d.) Crime Index by Country 2022. Retrieved from Numbeo: https://www.numbeo.com/crime/rankings_by_country.jsp?title=2022 (Accessed: 1st July 2022)

Numbeo (n.d.) Cost of Living Index by Country 2022. Retrieved from Numbeo: https://www.numbeo.com/cost-of-living/rankings_by_country.jsp?title=2022 (Accessed: 1st July 2022)

Numbeo (n.d.) Quality of Life Index by Country 2022. Retrieved from Numbeo: https://www.numbeo.com/quality-of-life/rankings_by_country.jsp?title=2022 (Accessed: 1st July 2022)

Numbeo (n.d.) Health Care Index by Country 2022. Retrieved from Numbeo: https://www.numbeo.com/health-care/rankings_by_country.jsp?title=2022 (Accessed: 1st July 2022)

Olympanalyt (n.d.) Olympic Games: results, medals, statistics, analytics Retrieved from Olympanalyt:

http://olympanalyt.com/OlympAnalytics.php?param_pagetype=MedalsByCountries&param_dbversion=&param_country=&param_games=ALL&param_sport=Snowboard (Accessed: 15th July 2022)

MacEacheran, M. (2018) The unlikely home of the world's smallest desert. Retrieved from BBC Travel: https://www.bbc.com/travel/article/20180621-the-unlikely-home-of-the-worlds-smallest-desert (Accessed: 15th July 2022)

MacDonald, T. (2020) You Can Try To Spot Whales From The Top Of The Tadoussac Dunes. Retrieved from MTL Blog: https://www.mtlblog.com/you-can-try-to-spot-whales-from-the-top-of-the-tadoussac-dunes (Accessed: 15th July 2022)

Atlas Obscura (2014) Great Sand Hills. Retrieved from Atlas Obscura: https://www.atlasobscura.com/places/great-sand-hills (Accessed: 15th July 2022)

Adele, J. (n.d.) Dunas de Bani Shenanigans. Retrieved from We Travel And Blog: https://wetravelandblog.com/2014/where-in-the-world/dunas-de-bani-shenanigans/ (Accessed: 15th July 2022)

Ministry of Tourism of Baja California (n.d.) Dunes - San Felipe, Baja California. Retrieved from San Felipe Travel: https://sanfelipe.travel/en/dunes/ (Accessed: 20th July 2022)

Volcano Discovery (2022) Cerro Negro Volcano, Nicaragua - Facts & Information. Retrieved from Volcano Discovery: https://www.volcanodiscovery.com/cerro_negro.html (Accessed: 20th July 2022)

Experience Pismo Beach (n.d.) Oceano Dunes. Retrieved from Pismo Beach Sand Dunes & Recreation Area: https://www.experiencepismobeach.com/beach-and-outdoors/oceano-dunes/ (Accessed: 24th July 2022)

National Park Service (n.d.) Sand Dunes - Death Valley National Park (U.S. National Park Service). Retrieved from National Park Service: https://www.nps.gov/deva/learn/nature/sand-dunes.htm (Accessed: 24th July 2022)

National Park Service (n.d.) Sandboarding and Sand Sledding - Great Sand Dunes National Park & Preserve Colorado. Retrieved from National Park Service: https://www.nps.gov/grsa/planyourvisit/sandboardingsandsledding.htm (Accessed: 24th July 2022)

Visit Utah (n.d.) Coral Pink Sand Dunes State Park. Retrieved from Utah Office of Tourism: https://www.visitutah.com/places-to-go/parks-outdoors/coral-pink-sand-dunes-state-park (Accessed: 24th July 2022)

Johnson, P. (n.d.) Sand Master Park. Retrieved from Oregon.com: https://www.oregon.com/attractions/sand-master-park (Accessed: 24th July 2022)

Original Travel (n.d.) The Biggest Sand Dunes in the World. Retrieved from Original Travel: https://www.originaltravel.co.uk/travel-blog/the-biggest-sand-dunes-in-the-world (Accessed: 25th July 2022)

Amboro Tours (n.d.) Lomas de Arena. Retrieved from Amboro Tours: https://www.amborotours.com/lomas-de-arena.html (Accessed: 31st July 2022)

Lost Towel Travels (2021) Local Approved Island Florianopolis Dunes And Best Beaches. Retrieved from Lost Towel Travel Adventures: https://losttoweltravels.com/florianopolis-dunes-and-beaches/ (Accessed: 31st July 2022)

Ribeiro, P. (2021) Lençóis Maranhenses National Park: The Complete Guide. Retrieved from Tripsavvy: https://www.tripsavvy.com/lencois-maranhenses-national-park-4172524 (Accessed: 31st July 2022)

Patowary, K. (2014) The Dragon Hill of Iquique, Chile. Retrieved from Amusing Planet: https://www.amusingplanet.com/2014/10/the-dragon-hill-of-iquique-chile.html (Accessed: 2nd August 2022)

Ecochile (2017) Visiting the driest desert on Earth - San Pedro de Atacama. Retrieved from Ecochile: https://ecochile.travel/san-pedro-de-atacama-visiting-driest-desert-earth/ (Accessed: 2nd August 2022)

Nicolson, N. (2015) Colombia's La Guajira Desert is attracting visitors. Retrieved from CNN Travel: https://edition.cnn.com/travel/article/colombia-desert-la-guajira/index.html (Accessed: 2nd August 2022)

Zenith Travel (2022) Palmira Desert. Retrieved from Zenith Travel: https://www.zenithecuador.com/blog/palmira-desert (Accessed: 4th August 2022)

Luna, M. (2021) 10 Stunning Facts About Peru's Massive Sand Dune Cerro Blanco. Retrieved from Homeschool Spanish Academy: https://www.spanish.academy/blog/10-stunning-facts-about-perus-massive-sand-dune-cerro-blanco/ (Accessed: 4th August 2022)

Auma, Q. (2022) Huacachina: This Charming Village In Peru Is Worth Visiting. Retrieved from The Travel: https://www.thetravel.com/why-visit-huacachina-peru/ (Accessed: 4th August 2022)

Ellis, D. (2019) Cabo Polonio, bona fide best of Uruguay. Retrieved from San Diego Reader: https://www.sandiegoreader.com/news/2019/feb/04/travel-cabo-polonio-best-uruguay/ (Accessed: 4th August 2022)

NASA Earth Observatory (n.d.) Venezuela's Sandy Peninsula. Retrieved from NASA Earth Observatory: https://earthobservatory.nasa.gov/images/148162/venezuelas-sandy-peninsula (Accessed: 4th August 2022)

Agathangelou, C. (2017) The Best Natural Wonders in Cyprus. Retrieved from The Culture Trip: https://theculturetrip.com/europe/cyprus/articles/the-top-10-natural-wonders-of-cyprus/ (Accessed: 6th August 2022)

Dora, V.D. (2022) Lighthouses: the solitary guards of the sea. Retrieved from Geographical: https://geographical.co.uk/culture/lighthouses-solitary-guards-of-the-sea (Accessed: 10th August 2022)

Lorelli, M. (2022) Did You Know Germany Has A Sand Ski Hill? Retrieved from Unofficial Networks: https://unofficialnetworks.com/2022/06/14/germany-ski-sand-hill/ (Accessed: 10th August 2022)

Zikakou, I. (2021) Lemnos: Home to Greece's Unique Desert. Retrieved from Greek Reporter: https://greekreporter.com/2021/04/07/lemnos-greece-unique-desert/ (Accessed: 10th August 2022)

Ó Conghaile, P. (2022) 10 best beaches in Ireland for 2022 – No.1 is an Irish family classic and here's why. Retrieved from Independent.ie: https://www.independent.ie/life/travel/awards/10-best-beaches-in-ireland-for-2022-no1-is-an-irish-family-classic-and-heres-why-41257684.html (Accessed: 14th August 2022)

Wright, R. (2021) Mount Etna: Everything you need to know about hiking up one of the world's most active volcanoes. Retrieved from Euronews: https://www.euronews.com/travel/2021/08/29/mount-etna-everything-you-need-to-know-about-hiking-up-one-of-the-world-s-most-active-volc (Accessed: 14th August 2022)

Atlas Obscura (2016) Moving Sand Dunes. Retrieved from Atlas Obscura: https://www.atlasobscura.com/places/moving-sand-dunes (Accessed: 14th August 2022)

Santos Sousa, F. (2022) Salir do Porto: the biggest dune in Portugal. Retrieved from Lisboa Secreta: https://lisboasecreta.co/salir-do-porto-a-maior-duna-de-portugal/ (Accessed: 14th August 2022)

Derzhavina, V. (2019) Moscow-area desert: sand dunes in Sychevo. Retrieved from Itinari: https://www.itinari.com/moscow-area-desert-sand-dunes-in-sychevo-g9n6 (Accessed: 17th August 2022)

Uppers (2022) Las cinco españolas que están entre las mejores de Europa. Retrieved from Uppers: https://www.uppers.es/estilo-de-vida/viajes/cinco-playas-espanolas-mejores-europa-be5ma_18_3312498210.html (Accessed: 17th August 2022)

Barceló Experiences (n.d.) Corralejo sand dunes: a small desert in Fuerteventura. Retrieved from Barceló Experiences: https://www.barcelo.com/guia-turismo/en/spain/fuerteventura/things-to-do/corralejo-sand-dunes/ (Accessed: 17th August 2022)

BBC (2022) North Devon first in UK to become World Surfing Reserve. Retrieved from BBC: https://www.bbc.co.uk/news/uk-england-devon-60979725 (Accessed: 17th August 2022)

Nation.Cymru (2022) The brilliant shirt designs for MLS style Welsh football league. Retrieved from Nation.Cymru: https://nation.cymru/sport/the-brilliant-shirt-designs-for-mls-style-welsh-football-league/ (Accessed: 17th August 2022)

The Press and Journal (2022) 11 of the best Aberdeenshire beaches for a day trip. Retrieved from The Press and Journal: https://www.pressandjournal.co.uk/fp/lifestyle/4573081/best-aberdeenshire-beaches-articleisfree/ (Accessed: 17th August 2022)

Guy, J. (2021) Camels get their own traffic signal in China. Retrieved from CNN: https://edition.cnn.com/travel/article/china-camel-traffic-lights-scli-intl/index.html (Accessed: 18th August 2022)

Xinhua (2022) Desert library offers unique experience in NW China's Ningxia Hui Autonomous Region. Retrieved from Global Times: https://www.globaltimes.cn/page/202207/1270312.shtml (Accessed: 18th August 2022)

Pang, K. (2021) Sand Sledging Around Beijing. Retrieved from China Highlights: https://www.chinahighlights.com/beijing/article-sand-sledging.htm (Accessed: 18th August 2022)

Daijiworld (2022) Places for senior citizens to enjoy. Retrieved from Daijiworld: https://daijiworld.com/news/newsDisplay?newsID=992672 (Accessed: 24th August 2022)

Tasnim News Agency (2019) Varzaneh Desert: One of the Most Beautiful Deserts in Iran. Retrieved from Tasnim News Agency: https://www.tasnimnews.com/en/news/2019/12/18/2161922/varzaneh-desert-one-of-the-most-beautiful-deserts-in-iran (Accessed: 31st August 2022)

Gholami, M. (2020) Rig-e Zarin Desert. Retrieved from Persia Planet: http://persiaplanet.com/rig-e-zarin-desert/ (Accessed: 31st August 2022)

Christofaro, B. (2019) Sand Graffiti: Japan Angry at Tourists for Writing Messages into Dunes. Retrieved from Insider: https://www.insider.com/sand-graffiti-japan-angry-at-tourists-for-writing-messages-into-dunes-2019-5 (Accessed: 19th September 2022)

Bakht, S. (2022) Driving the King's Highway through Jordan. Retrieved from The Times: https://www.thetimes.co.uk/article/driving-the-kings-highway-through-jordan-92v9300d6 (Accessed: 21st September 2022)

Bulatkulova, S. (2021) Kazakh National Geography Society Unveils Charyn Canyon and Altyn Emel National Parks Development Plans. Retrieved from The Astana Times: https://astanatimes.com/2021/09/kazakh-national-geography-society-unveils-charyn-canyon-and-altyn-emel-national-parks-development-plans/ (Accessed: 21st September 2022)

Veldwijk, I. (2020) Melaka Desert – Sauntering About the Shifting Sand Dunes at Sunset. Retrieved from Mind of a Hitchhiker: https://mindofahitchhiker.com/melaka-desert-sauntering-shifting-sand-dunes-sunset/ (Accessed: 28th September 2022)

Bhatia, A. (2022) Mongolia's 10 Must-See Natural Wonders. Retrieved from The Travel: https://www.thetravel.com/natural-wonders-in-mongolia/ (Accessed: 28th September 2022)

Amar, N. (2022) The 8 best places to visit in Oman. Retrieved from Lonely Planet: https://www.lonelyplanet.com/articles/best-places-to-visit-in-oman (Accessed: 5th October 2022)

Adriano, L. (2022) Paoay sand dunes art installation boosts Ilocos Norte tourism. Retrieved from Philippine News Agency: https://www.pna.gov.ph/articles/1179256 (Accessed: 9th October 2022)

Thompson, N. (2022) Best Qatar activites for World Cup football fans. Retrieved from Mirror: https://www.mirror.co.uk/travel/qatar-activities-world-cup-football-26468550 (Accessed: 9th October 2022)

Hürriyet Daily News (2017) Antalya's Patara Beach draws tourists with dunes. Retrieved from Hürriyet Daily News: https://www.hurriyetdailynews.com/antalyas-patara-beach-draws-tourists-with-dunes--111640 (Accessed: 10th October 2022)

TRT (2022) Știați că în Turcia există un deșert? Retrieved from TRT: https://www.trt.net.tr/romana/programe/2022/05/20/politica-turciei-cu-privire-la-nato-1829962 (Accessed: 15th October 2022)

Romanov, D. (n.d.) Sand Dunes of Archer. Retrieved from Socotra.info: https://socotra.info/sand-dunes-of-archer.html (Accessed: 15th October 2022)

Mason, B. (2009) Sublime Sand: Desert Dunes Seen From Space. Retrieved from Wired: https://www.wired.com/2009/12/deserts-gallery-1/ (Accessed: 17th October 2022)

Mathala, S. (2022) A Weekend of Fun At Khawa Dune Challenge. Retrieved from The Voice: https://news.thevoicebw.com/a-weekend-of-fun-at-khawa-dune-challenge/ (Accessed: 17th October 2022)

Canning, A. (2022) Best things to do in Cape Verde. Retrieved from The Times: https://www.thetimes.co.uk/travel/destinations/africa/cape-verde/best-things-to-do-in-cape-verde (Accessed: 17th October 2022)

Begin North Adventures (n.d.) Loibor Seder Kenya's Biggest Sand Dune. Retrieved from Begin North Adventures: https://beginnorthadventures.com/loibor-seder-sand-dune-kenya/ (Accessed: 18th October 2022)

Rahmoun, A. (2021) Dune-fixing in Madagascar: A line in the sand for extreme weather. Retrieved from World Food Programme: https://www.wfp.org/stories/dune-fixing-madagascar-line-sand-extreme-weather (Accessed: 24th October 2022)

Casey, M. (2015) Scientists Debate Evidence of Ancient Megatsunami. Retrieved from National Geographic: https://www.nationalgeographic.com/science/article/151221-ancient-megatsunami-madagascar-debate-science (Accessed: 24th October 2022)

Khrustaleva, O. (2020) Chinguetti: Mauritania's ancient Saharan city. Retrieved from BBC Travel: https://www.bbc.com/travel/article/20200709-chinguetti-mauritanias-ancient-saharan-city (Accessed: 24th October 2022)

Taylor, E. (2022) Mozambique's Kisawa Sanctuary Is the African Beach Holiday You've Been Dreaming Of. Retrieved from Vogue: https://www.vogue.com/article/mozambique-kisawa-sanctuary-beach-holiday (Accessed: 26th October 2022)

Fox News (2018) World's record-breaking sand dunes. Retrieved from Fox News: https://www.foxnews.com/travel/worlds-record-breaking-sand-dunes (Accessed: 26th October 2022)

Zaino, L. (2022) 10 of the most underrated vacation destinations in Africa. Retrieved from The Points Guy: https://thepointsguy.com/guide/africa-underrated-vacation-places/ (Accessed: 26th October 2022)

Yotamara, U.C. (2022) Exploring The Magical Elan Of Yusufari Sand Dunes. Retrieved from New Telegraph: https://www.newtelegraphng.com/exploring-the-magical-elan-of-yusufari-sand-dunes/ (Accessed: 29th October 2022)

Good, R. (2022) Senegal: Travel Content Creator Dev Walker Shares Her Favorite Places To Visit. Retrieved from Forbes: https://www.forbes.com/sites/ranagood/2022/06/21/senegal-travel-content-creator-dev-walker-shares-her-favorite-places-to-visit/?sh=3c5ae1d15002 (Accessed: 2nd November 2022)

Dragon Dune Sandboarding (n.d.) Dragon Dune. Retrieved from Dragon Dune Sandboarding: https://dragondune.com/ (Accessed: 9th November 2022)

St. Lucia (n.d.) St. Lucia. Retrieved from St Lucia SA: http://www.stluciasa.co.za/sl_home.htm (Accessed: 9th November 2022)

Johnstone, H. (2018) Can Tunisia revive its tourist industry? Retrieved from Financial Times: https://www.ft.com/content/ce1f38b8-8f5c-11e8-9609-3d3b945e78cf (Accessed: 15th November 2022)

Gervais, E. (2022) Tunisia Is The Land of Sea and Sand. Retrieved from Elle: https://www.ellecanada.com/culture/travel/tunisia-is-the-land-of-sea-and-sand (Accessed: 15th November 2022)

Bumidin, Q. (2022) 7 Best Road Trips From Perth For The Best Self-Drive Vacation (From 30 Mins to 21 Hours). Retrieved from HaveHalalWillTravel: https://www.havehalalwilltravel.com/road-trip-from-perth-western-australia (Accessed: 16th November 2022)

Smithson, B. (2022) How Kangaroo Island recovered from Australia's devastating bush fires and a global pandemic. Retrieved from The Points Guy: https://thepointsguy.co.uk/news/kangaroo-island-bushfire-recovery/ (Accessed: 16th November 2022)

Tang, P. (2022) 23 unmissable things to do in Australia. Retrieved from Lonely Planet: https://www.lonelyplanet.com/articles/top-things-to-do-in-australia (Accessed: 16th November 2022)

Sunder, K. (2022) A shore winner: Beauty of Australian coastlines. Retrieved from The New Indian Express: https://www.newindianexpress.com/lifestyle/travel/2022/aug/28/a-shore-winner-beauty-of-australian-coastlines-2491792.html (Accessed: 18th November 2022)

Sinclair, S. (2022) How to make a rainbow connection with nature. Retrieved from Sunshine Coast News: https://www.sunshinecoastnews.com.au/2022/02/11/how-to-make-a-rainbow-connection-with-nature/ (Accessed: 18th November 2022)

Pengilley, V. (2022) Birdsville Big Red Bash features 'spontaneous' outback wedding. Retrieved from ABC News: https://www.abc.net.au/news/2022-07-07/big-red-bash-spontaneous-outback-wedding/101213390 (Accessed: 18th November 2022)

Shepert, E. (2022) Vancover flights: Cheap trip to Fiji and how to save there. Retrieved from Vancouver Is Awesome: https://www.vancouverisawesome.com/travel/google-flights-vancouver-yvr-fiji-nadi-destination-6011018 (Accessed: 20th November 2022)

Pollok, S. (2022) New Zealand ranked second most beautiful country in the world. Retrieved from NZ Herald: https://www.nzherald.co.nz/travel/new-zealand-ranked-second-most-beautiful-country-in-the-world/LPWKDK5ANM4JLA65Q3UL3H3EUI/ (Accessed: 20th November 2022)

Spodyneiko, K (2020) The big trio of Northland. Retrieved from Focus: https://focusmagazine.co.nz/the-big-trio-of-northland-cape-reinga-90-mile-beach-and-te-paki-sand-dunes/ (Accessed: 20th November 2022)

Karryon (2022) You've got hot mail: Vanuatu's Mt Yasur Volcano post box is back in action. Retrieved from Karryon: https://karryon.com.au/lifestyle/youve-got-hot-mail-vanuatus-mt-yasur-volcano-post-box-is-back-in-action/ (Accessed: 20th November 2022)

www.ingramcontent.com/pod-product-compliance
Lightning Source LLC
Chambersburg PA
CBHW041138110526
44590CB00027B/4060